SHAKESPEARE AND TWENTIETH-CENTURY IRISH DRAMA

For my parents

Shakespeare and Twentieth-Century Irish Drama
Conceptualizing Identity and Staging Boundaries

REBECCA STEINBERGER
College Misericordia, USA

Routledge
Taylor & Francis Group
LONDON AND NEW YORK

First published 2008 by Ashgate Publishing

Reissued 2018 by Routledge
2 Park Square, Milton Park, Abingdon, Oxon, OX14 4RN
711 Third Avenue, New York, NY 10017, USA

Routledge is an imprint of the Taylor & Francis Group, an informa business

First issued in paperback 2018

A Library of Congress record exists under LC control number: 2007021920

Notice:
Product or corporate names may be trademarks or registered trademarks, and are used only for identification and explanation without intent to infringe.

Publisher's Note
The publisher has gone to great lengths to ensure the quality of this reprint but points out that some imperfections in the original copies may be apparent.

Disclaimer
The publisher has made every effort to trace copyright holders and welcomes correspondence from those they have been unable to contact.

ISBN 13: 978-0-815-39701-4 (hbk)
ISBN 13: 978-1-138-62053-7 (pbk)
ISBN 13: 978-1-351-14928-0 (ebk)

Contents

Acknowledgments

There are many individuals and institutions which have helped make this project a reality. Throughout my academic career, I've had inspiring mentors and friends who have influenced and shaped my teaching and scholarship in a variety of ways. Stanley Gutin, Benjamin Fiester, Thomas Kaska, Bruce Auerbach, Michael Friedman, and Stephen Whittaker—many thanks for laying the groundwork in my intellectual development. I am especially indebted to Christopher Orchard, whose insight in the early stages of this scholarship has impacted this study immensely. In addition, Malcolm Hayward, Robert Andrew Wilson, and Thaer Al-Kadi offered extremely helpful feedback in earlier drafts. Allan Austin, Corine Coniglio and Tricia Zakreski also deserve thanks for providing moral support.

I am so grateful for the support from the College Misericordia community, and especially the English Department, as well as the Faculty Development Committee for awarding me Summer Research Grants. These grants funded my research trips to do archival work at the British Library, London, and the Trinity College Library, Dublin, in 2001 and 2002. Many thanks also go out to the amicable staff of the Rare Books and Music Reading Room at the British Library as well as the library staff at Trinity College Dublin, College Misericordia, and Indiana University of Pennsylvania. I also wish to acknowledge Seamus Deane and Field Day for providing me with the images concerning the premiere of Brian Friel's play *Translations*.

To my student Research Assistants at Misericordia, I thank you for your attention to detail and willingness to assist in oftentimes tedious and detailed technology-related issues. Marianna Fiorini, Rianna Johns, Trista Bratlee, Christian Beck, Dennis Hando, Wendy Carey, Jacob Garner, Michael O'Connor, Michael Marr, Sara Bray, and Ryan Balara—I thank you sincerely. Thanks for all of the coffees!

My editor, Ann Donahue, deserves many thanks, as do the anonymous reviewers for Ashgate who provided helpful comments that allowed me to improve the focal point of this book. Without the copyediting skills and careful reading of Thomas P. Balázs, I'd still be revising this. Part of Chapter 3 was previously published in *Núa: Studies in Contemporary Irish Writing*, and I thank the editors for their kind permission to reprint a portion of that article. I have presented pieces of this text at a number of conferences and am especially grateful to Joshua Fisher, Jad Smith, Adam Cohen, David Hawkes, Mark Aune, and D J. Hopkins for their crucial feedback and, more importantly, their friendship. Thanks also to the Manuscripts Department at Trinity College Dublin for permission to use the cover illustration.

Most importantly, I wish to thank my always encouraging family. The unwavering support and guidance of Annunciata Lepore, Helen Steinberger, Louise and Jim Fisk, and Robert and Darlene Steinberger made my academic pursuits a reality. In particular, my parents, Robert and Marie Steinberger, to whom this book is dedicated with love, continue to be my biggest supporters. I am truly blessed.

List of Plates

Introduction

Since the publication of Edward Said's seminal work *Orientalism* (1978), postcolonial studies has surfaced as a major critical movement investigating the treatment of marginalized factions (known as the Other) by their oppressors. As such, important evaluative approaches to literature which encompasses colonialism have followed, and even questioned, Said. While Said and early postcolonial critics initially discussed the Other as a Western construct of Eastern identity, the relationship between colonizer and colonized is also applicable to Western cultures that have been objectified by hegemonic practices.[1] The ramifications of colonialism have been addressed at length in terms of the relationship between Ireland and England. While diverse studies have linked Shakespeare with postcolonialism,[2] England's famed writer is often indicted as being a model for hegemonic discourse in the Renaissance.[3] But what many studies have failed to argue is the way in which Shakespeare actually provides a voice to the Other in his plays, and how—in doing so—oppressed cultures assimilate his anti-colonial writings as a means of asserting their own voices.

The following study specifically explores Shakespeare's influence on the dramatic genre in Ireland through an examination of two representative Irish writers, modern dramatist Sean O'Casey and contemporary playwright Brian Friel. In addition, I explain how, through reinscriptions of Shakespeare's drama in their own works, and particularly through interpretations of *1 Henry IV*, *2 Henry IV*, and *Henry V*, their plays precipitated a wave of national identity in Irish drama of the Modern and Contemporary periods. Although critics have long placed Shakespeare within the hegemonic discourse of the West, this examination argues that his works represent—and have been recognized by Irish writers as—the voice of the Other as he attempts to move the colonized (previously categorized as the Object) into the position of the Subject—a category usually occupied by hegemonic forces of the past and present.

To address the problems concerning Shakespeare's relation to colonialism, his plays must be discussed in relation to first, their historical context in Elizabethan

---

[1]   See Said's chapter on 'Yeats and Decolonization' in *Culture and Imperialism. New York:* Vintage, 1993.

[2]   Ania Loomba suggests, 'it is more helpful to think of postcolonialism not just as coming literally after colonialism and signifying its demise, but more flexibly as the contestation of colonial domination and the legacies of colonialism ... It also allows us to incorporate the history of anti-colonial resistance with contemporary resistances to imperialism and dominant Western culture.' *Colonialism/Postcolonialism.* London and New York: Routledge, 1998. 12.

[3]   Willy Maley. *Nation, State and Empire in English Renaissance Literature: Shakespeare to Milton.* New York: Palgrave, 2003. 58.

England and second, to their nationalistic values as part of the imperialist ideology of European nations. I argue that Shakespeare needs to be read as part of an anti-colonial discourse. Chapter 1 addresses these notions and also enables a more specific literary comparison between Shakespeare and Edmund Spenser, whose *A View of the Present State of Ireland* reflects a dominant ideology of England in the late sixteenth century. More specifically, Spenser's text serves as an agenda of deterritorialization and dispossession through its flagrant stereotypes of the Irish people and their geographical space. Chapter 1 highlights the question of national identity invoked by Macmorris, the first Irish character on the English stage, whose presence in *Henry V* serves to provoke analysis of the Irish question in the British Empire. My purpose in doing so is to illuminate the potential for Irish playwrights, some four hundred years later, to appropriate Shakespeare's embodiment of the emergent cultural identity for themselves. These Irish playwrights use Shakespeare, the foremost English dramatist, to demonstrate the cultural schizophrenia of a colonized Ireland competing against English hegemony. What makes this study particularly innovative is not only the articulation of how one culture reads itself in the discourse of an(O)ther, but also the radical implications of Irish writers using the tools of the English hegemony to define themselves. As seen through *Richard II*, Shakespeare challenges the rhetoric of the dominant ideology and, therefore, exposes the malignancy of imperialism. This is the very reason why Shakespeare is reconstructed by Irish dramatists.

Drawing from Chapter 1's understanding of the Subject/Object relationship between England/Ireland, Chapter 2 considers the efforts forged by the Abbey Theatre in Dublin to create an emerging discourse independent from the oppressor. Led primarily by William Butler Yeats and Lady Augusta Gregory, the Abbey showcased Irish playwrights with Irish words on an Irish stage. This creation of an uniquely Irish theatrical project was well received at the dawn of the twentieth century. However, this chapter considers the sometimes turbulent productions staged during this politically charged epoch in Ireland with an analysis of the Playboy and Plough Riots that occurred during the premieres of J.M. Synge's *The Playboy of the Western World* and Sean O'Casey's *The Plough and the Stars*, respectively. Despite the professed apoliticism of the Abbey directorate, the urban/rural binary of the audience resulted in linguistic and cultural miscommunication and, hence, the riots reflected these misconceptions. My study differs from the historical treatment of the Abbey in that it examines the counter-hegemonic surgence sparked by the Irish literati. Conversely, a dominant ideology would have the theatre pacify a population rather than awaken them to how that hegemony constructs them. In addition, I stress the theatre's response to political upheavals manifested in its productions that deal with the events themselves—the Easter Rising of 1916, the Irish Civil War of 1922—and the Irish statesman who incited volunteers to fight against imperial domination, Padraic Pearse. What is particularly fascinating is the interweaving of politics and art, a point which surfaces again in Chapter 3.

Picking up with Sean O'Casey, the eminent playwright of the Abbey, I investigate the interconnectivity of Shakespeare's *Henriad* and the Dublin dramatist's *Juno and the Paycock* and *The Plough and the Stars* which consider the social, sexual, and nationalist tensions concerning the Civil War in Ireland and the 1916 Rising. In particular, this examination uncovers elements of Shakespeare used to characterize an Irish nationality under the supposed apoliticism of the Abbey's Board of Directors. By using Shakespeare as an ideological model, Sean O'Casey subverts both the English hegemony and the Abbey Theatre's apoliticism by modeling his Irish characters on English terms. Through O'Casey's *Juno* and *Plough*, this chapter establishes a direct link from the present Irish turmoils to those four hundred years earlier as articulated in Shakespeare's plays.

Corresponding with the analysis of the Abbey Theatre, Chapter 3 investigates the polypolitical agenda of the Field Day Theatre Company which was established in 1980 in Northern Ireland. Founded by dramatist Brian Friel and actor Stephen Rea, this enterprise included Seamus Heaney, Tom Paulin, David Hammond, and Seamus Deane. Similar to the Abbey, the Field Day Board of Directors planned to create a theatre that would promote an emergent artistic vision for the Irish; but unlike the Abbey, the focus was not on the urban center of Dublin. Rather, the Field Day placed its energies in the North of Ireland which had been long-neglected. In addition to staging plays relevant to Irish identity—which again reiterate the question proposed by Macmorris as addressed in Chapter 1—this artistic venture also published pamphlets, constructed the 'fifth province' to promote Irish intelligentsia distinct from England, and published a first-ever anthology of Irish writing. These efforts resisted stereotyping and identification with English hegemonic intellectual circles. But more profoundly, the Field Day Theatre Company created a cultural space for Northern Ireland.

Finally, this inquiry considers the questions regarding identity raised in Chapter 1 through an analysis of Brian Friel's *Translations* and his appropriation of Shakespeare's *Henriad*. I contend that Friel takes the Irish question and gaelicizes the issues inherent in the struggle for a national identity. Differing from the O'Casey plays considered in relation to the *Henriad* in Chapter 2, Friel's play (the first production of the Field Day Theatre Company) focuses on a major historical event that occurred in County Donegal in the 1830s and sparked the Irish erasure. In doing so he articulates how the Ordnance Survey, instituted by the British Empire, incited the deculturation of Ireland, the erosion of its language, and the dispossession of the people. By appropriating Shakespeare's issues with the Celtic Other in the *Henriad*, Friel also subverts English hegemony.

My main focus is to elucidate how Shakespeare's plays—which stage elements of history and nationalism—are resurrected, rewritten, and reinscribed in twentieth-century Irish drama. In doing so, I show how Irish dramatists have appropriated Shakespeare as a reaction to the language of the imperialist discourse in order to reconceptualize their position and support their revision of the Irish as Subject.

Chapter 1

'What Ish My Nation?': The Blurring of National Identity in Shakespeare's *Henry V*, *Richard II*, and Spenser's *A View Of The Present State Of Ireland*

Elizabethan political ideology incites colonial enterprises through the use of propaganda writings in which pamphleteers construct denigrating images of Ireland and its people. This trend was also carried out in literature which served to establish a dominant discourse that would privilege England over Other cultures. In particular, Edmund Spenser's *A View of the Present State of Ireland* deals a damaging blow to England's Western neighbor through the use of linguistic tactics which perpetuate these stereotypes. However, this colonial servant is censured by his antithetical contemporary, William Shakespeare, whose history play *Richard II* exposes Spenser's plan of deterritorialization by critiquing an Elizabethan foreign policy that supports imperial domination. In addition to this critique, Shakespeare then shows through *Henry V* that English national identity is not achieved through 'Englishness,' but rather through the oppression of the Other. This approach suggests how it is possible to read Shakespeare against state-supported hegemonic writings such as Spenser's *View*.

When addressing the 'Irish question,' the tenuous relationship between Ireland and England of this past century comes to mind—with the media's sensationalizing of IRA activity in Northern Ireland and devastating bombings as a result of this ancient conflict, it is difficult to pinpoint where the hostility between these island neighbors began. But what is largely misunderstood as a religious conflict has actually been in existence since the twelfth century.[1] After Henry VIII declared himself King of Ireland in 1541, ill sentiments spread rapidly throughout Great Britain. But it was not until the late 1500s when Elizabeth I—who was well aware of Catholic Spain's interest in the isle—began to transplant English nobility onto Irish soil that the Irish question became truly pronounced.[2] As a result, numerous pamphlets and tracts

---

[1]   Misconceptions of Ireland in the late twelfth century stemmed from the writings of Giraldus Cambrensis, *Topographia Hiberniae* (c. 1187) and *Expugnatio Hiberniae* (c. 1189).

[2]   For an extensive study on this relationship, see D.B. Quinn, *The Elizabethans and the Irish*. Ithaca, NY: Cornell UP, 1966.

laden with propaganda permeated England and sustained the stereotyping of the Irish nation and its people.[3] The resulting socio-political chaos, I believe, was the direct result of the blurred boundaries of a national identity that existed and persisted through England's campaign of assimilation. By indicating a 'blurring' of identities here, I am positing that the Irish national identity—which is not fixed—at times becomes indistinguishable from the English identity that continually seeks to define itself through marginalization of the Other.

Disseminating Identity: England's Sense of Self and the Irish Other

By examining the numerous linguistic devices that operate to position one discourse over another, we can better assess Elizabethan England's imperialist agenda and quest for territorial gain. Political tracts, propaganda-laden pamphlets, and popular literature of the era contained the colonial biases that helped perpetuate damaging stereotypes of cultures relegated to the periphery in this dominant discourse.[4] Additionally, visual culture—chiefly through the art of mapmaking—led its own brand of hegemony,[5] as it re-oriented the image of nations, cultures, and peoples in the Renaissance. Following Christopher Saxton's production of an *Atlas of England and Wales* in 1579[6] and the defeat of the Spanish Armada in 1588, England's image as a Western powerhouse was bolstered by its depiction in maps and through the documents that position the land as central to the discourse of the dominant social order. For that reason, the visual and linguistic manifestation of chorography (the depiction of a specific region or territory) functioned in the construction of geographic space. Imperial agents subverted the territories they desired to control by manipulating the chorography of maps as depicted through John Norden's *Speculum Britannia* (1598) and surveying tracts like Ralph Agas's *A Preparative to Plotting of Landes and Tenements for surveigh*. In the latter, Agas warns the reader of the potential for abuse with land surveying: 'The practice hereof ... is but new, and scarsely established ...[I]t were then an exceeding losse to the common weale, a dangerous harming of [peace] ... if this excellent practice should be overthrowne

---

³   According to Shelia T. Cavanagh, Ireland's rebellion 'reached crisis proportions during Elizabeth I's reign and numerous English writers—the most renowned being Edmund Spenser—struggled to provide reasons and solutions for the increasing chaos'. '"The Fatal Destiny of the Land": Elizabethan Views on Ireland.' *Representing Ireland: Literature and the Origins of Conflict, 1534–1660.* Ed. Brendan Bradshaw, Andrew Hadfield, and Willy Maley. Cambridge: Cambridge UP, 1993. 116.

⁴   See, for example, John Bale's *Vocacyon* (1553), Edmund Campion's *A History of Ireland* (1571), Sir Philip Sidney's *Discourse on Irish Affairs* (1571), Barnabe Rich's *A New Description of Ireland* (1610), and *An Itinerary* (1617) by Fynes Moryson.

⁵   For a detailed history of the depiction of Ireland in maps, see J.H. Andrews, *Shapes of Ireland: Maps and Their Makers 1564–1839.* Dublin: Geography Publications, 1997.

⁶   The year 1579 marks the preoccupation with the map as visual signifier of England's national identity.

and destroid by abusing the same.'[7] This illustration therefore reveals the potential for chorography of England's geographic space to be exaggerated by politicos and literati alike as a means of locating the nation's cultural epi-center as a prime territory for mercantilism and commerce. In fact, Robert Payne discloses that 'the generall Map of Ireland, which is joined with the old Map of England, is most false: The author (as it seemeth) drew them both by reporte, and the common computation of myles ... and the Mappe of Ireland littell more then one forth at that if would be, if it were truly drawen.'[8] What Payne alludes to in this tract, then, was not an anomaly. By historicizing specific texts published in late-1500s England, we can assess how the mapping of space operated to construct a national identity at the onset of the defining moment of English nationalism.

The effect of new technologies, including surveying, on ideologies of land use and settlement must be considered in understanding England's concept of the nation as a distinctive landscape. The textual manifestations of landscape (or space) thus contained ideological, territorial, and subjective shaping of new colonies. While in England, the concept of rural space infers breaking the confines of city/civility/court life (as evidenced in Shakespeare's plays *As You Like It*, *A Midsummer Night's Dream*, and Sir Philip Sidney's *Arcadia*), cartographers and/or surveyors subvert this same space in marginalized nations to minimize their potency. Ireland, in particular, was subject to this deterritorialization which resulted in the subsequent erosion of Irish culture.

How does literature in Elizabethan England successfully construct its own map of authority? As Nicholas Canny suggests, 'Almost every English-born author writing of Ireland during the 1580s and 1590s was insistent upon the development of a clearly-defined radical programme of reform which would involve the erection of a completely new commonwealth upon firm foundations.'[9] At the same time land surveying was becoming an important tool in shaping England's rural/urban space (the town and country, if you will), Edmund Spenser's *A View of the Present State of Ireland* was published (1596). Contemporary students of Elizabethan England would recognize Spenser as a model of English nationalism, but perhaps few might recognize him as a colonial official. It is my contention that Spenser did much damage to Ireland through his *View* by offering Elizabeth and imperial strategists the impetus for colonizing Ireland. But how was this possible? Spenser was known for his prose and poetry, but he was not schooled in cartography. Yet, the literary map of Ireland established in *View* is drawn with an authority that reduces Irish space to an 'uncivil,' 'desolate' 'wasteland.' Even more intriguing is the immediate function of the exiled Spenser's sketch; for he indicts Elizabeth as being weak in her program of

---

[7]   Ralph Agas. *A Preparative to Plotting of Landes and Tenements for surveigh, shewing the Diversitie of sundrie instruments supplied thereunto.* London, 1596. 6.

[8]   Richard Helgerson. *Forms of Nationhood: The Elizabethan Writings of England.* Chicago: University of Chicago Press, 1992. 112.

[9]   Nicholas Canny. 'Edmund Spenser and the Development of an Anglo-Irish Identity.' *Yearbook of English Studies* 13 (1983): 7.

hegemony over Ireland. This indictment embedded in the dialogue between Eudoxus and Irenius carries a warning, also, as Elizabeth is cognizant of Catholic Spain's interest in England's island neighbor.

Spenser is not the first Elizabethan to link the Queen with geographic space; nor is he the most prominent.[10] Cartographers inscribed their maps with recognizable symbols—such as the royal coat of arms—and even Elizabeth herself, who appears on the frontispiece to Saxton's atlas (1579), for example. But nowhere is Elizabeth's relation to the geographical space she rules more evident than in the Ditchley portrait (1592). The illustration of Elizabeth standing on Saxton's map implies that the two are inextricably linked—Elizabeth *is* a representation of the land itself[11] ... politically, metaphorically, and visually. Spenser seemingly draws on this—in *A View* as well as in *Faerie Queene*—to both praise his sovereign and warn her.

In his important study, Richard Helgerson asserts that 'maps do not ... speak only of the source of their authority—that is, of the power that through the system of patronage brought them into existence—but also of the relation of that power to the land they depict.'[12] Thus, taking a cue from the art of cartography, Spenser, too, transfers England's power over Ireland with an air of authority. As a royal servant, Spenser was dispatched to County Cork to establish colonial order and oversee English plantations, or 'plots.' His growing dissatisfaction (as mentioned earlier) with England's imperial enterprise in Ireland resulted in *A View of the Present State of Ireland* and therefore, mapping the Other as a means of asserting/inserting English hegemony.

How Does a Text 'Colonize'?

According to sixteenth-century historians, while Spain desired Ireland for her own means, Elizabeth warned the Spanish crown that she considered 'Ireland part of the English crown, a legacy of her ancestors' and that she was quite prepared to defend 'her properties.'[13] Thus, a heightened period of anxiety launched an influx of English officials taking up residence in Ireland. More importantly, the presence of the English on Irish ground—represented by a dichotomy between individuals with Old English ideals and those who fall in the category of the New English[14]—led to a deeper inquiry

---

[10] For a detailed analysis of this issue, see Christopher Highley's 'The Royal Image in Elizabethan Ireland' in *Dissing Elizabeth: Negative Representations of Gloriana*. Ed. Julia M. Walker. Durham and London: Duke UP, 1990. 60–76.

[11] Robert Payne. *A Brife Description of Ireland*. London: Thomas Dawson, 1590. 5.

[12] Helgerson. *Forms of Nationhood*, 111.

[13] See Juan E. Tazón-Salces, 'Politics, Literature and Colonization: A View of Ireland in the Sixteenth Century.' *Dutch Quarterly Review of Anglo-American Letters* 18.3 (1988): 186–98.

[14] Barnabe Rich denounces the English monarch in several tracts; and Christopher Highley notes that the colonial servant's undermining of Elizabethan policy in Ireland and 'his disgust at her preference for pardons over punishment' was universal among a number

of what constitutes a 'national' identity. As evidenced in Elizabethan pamphlets, the New English often charged Elizabeth's Irish policy as weak. Dissatisfaction with Elizabeth's sensitivity to Old English opinion and her reluctance to prosecute large-scale war was widespread among the faction of colonial servants who took up posts in Ireland from the mid-1500s. While Spenser was not the only open social critic of the body politic, his ideology differs from that of other colonial discourses because it creates a prototype for total assimilation of the Irish space.[15] Spenser understood the possible ramifications for the Elizabethan court if the pursuit of Ireland was not a primary military and political focus.[16] In fact, his main motivation for writing *View* was a 'response to Queen Elizabeth's vacillating and placatory policies in dealing with the Irish question.'[17] The text thus serves to delineate the variances of Spenser's foreign policy as compared to the Queen's, and I believe it is important that Spenser would not be afforded the ability to voice his own plan for colonization had he been living in England under Elizabeth's direct scrutiny.

In Spenser's *View*, he offers a dialogue between two characters, Eudoxus and Irenius, who exchange reductive judgments with regard to sundry affairs in Ireland. Not only does he find fault with the land, but he imposes a cultural alienation of the race when he intimates that there was never a Celtic-speaking people and the Spaniard is ethnically impure.[18] In doing so, the writer downplays Spanish claims on the island and paints Ireland as a barren territory that lacks a definitive culture and history. Spenser's *View* illustrates the author's specific intent to validate England's imperial enterprise there. As the text asserts, Spenser's designs include imposing a political hegemony over Ireland, and these intentions are couched in metaphors targeting England as the physician that the 'diseased patient'—Ireland— needs. Throughout this dialogue, Spenser repeatedly reduces Ireland to an 'uncivil' and 'desolate' 'wasteland,' and the inhabitants are stigmatized as 'savage,' 'barbarians,' and 'the very wild Irish.' Clearly, the repetition of these metaphors operates to inscribe a distorted and cynical portrait of the land and its people and marginalize

---

of political propagandists—including Spenser. Furthermore, Highley asserts that the 'dissing' of Elizabeth in Ireland was as much a part of a collective New English discourse as it was of the words and deeds of her declared Irish enemies, 71. See 'The Royal Image in Elizabethan Ireland' in *Dissing Elizabeth: Negative Representations of Gloriana*. Ed. Julia M. Walker. Durham, NC and London: Duke UP, 1998. 60–76.

[15]   Walter S.H. Lim. 'Figuring Justice: Imperial Ideology and the Discourse of Colonialism in Book V of *The Faerie Queene* and *A View of the Present State of Ireland.*' *Renaissance and Reformation* 19.1 (1995): 45–70.

[16]   As Lim articulates, 'Spenser believed Elizabeth had failed to intervene decisively and free the Low Countries from oppression by Catholic Spain. That the Queen did not give her uncompromising support to combat the threat posed by Catholic Spain and the Hapsburg powers in Europe proved scandalous to the militant Protestants ... Spenser was drawn to the larger international concerns of the reformed religion. And like Essex, he would like to have seen Elizabeth pursue a more interventionist and militant foreign policy' (49–50).

[17]   Lim. 'Figuring Justice.' 61.

[18]   Lim. 'Figuring Justice.' 58.

the Irish. Not only does Spenser paint an unstable picture of Ireland when he asserts that England is 'the cure' to 'redress' Ireland, for 'fear that it might lapse into its former condition,'[19] but Irenius's reference to 'Irish deserts'[20] and a 'goodly country wasted and left desolate'[21] imagines the land as fruitless. This is precisely how deterritorialization, the process whereby a dominant faction assumes control of a territory and, during this possession, strips it of its former inhabitants, operates in colonial discourse. Plantations function to assimilate—the territory, the people, the culture—and make them more effective (or in Spenser's case, more English).

Spenser utilizes topographical elements in the colonial text to propel feelings of unity and disunity and bring Ireland into an existence suited to the New English view. The linguistic map of Ireland he offers here provides a not-so-subtle commentary on Elizabethan policy; for Eudoxus states, 'it is a great wilfulness in any such landlord, to refuse to make any longer farms unto their tenants, as may besides the general good of the realm, be also greatly for their own profit and avail.'[22] While Spenser focuses on profit for both landlords of the Irish rural space, he negates the Irish people's capability to 'farm' their own territory. Geographical space appears to be important in defining the nation as its own individualized entity, and through Spenser's gradual erasure of Ireland's autonomy, he positions England as landlord over her 'tenement.' Juxtaposing his native country to the one he now finds himself in, Spenser's Eudoxus makes it clear that England—and Elizabeth—must intervene and prevent Ireland from 'falling into some other more dangerous than it.'[23] In sum, Spenser's biased text yields the rural space of Ireland as diseased and at the same time reinforces England's privileged position of authority in contrast.

Additional metaphors of disease indicate a layered erosion of Irish space and suggest the underlying mentality of hegemonic forces. For example, when Eudoxus inquires how Ireland can be reformed if not through 'laws and ordinances'—and Spenser is referring to 'English' modes of order, of course—Irenius warns that 'all those evils must be first cut away with a strong hand before any good can be planted, like as the corrupt branches and the unwholesome boughs are first to be pruned, and the foul moss cleansed or scraped away,[24] before the tree can bring forth any good fruit.'[25] The interesting point here is that Spenser is concerned *first* with geographical issues rather than policy—and this is not to suggest that the two are mutually

---

[19]   Edmund Spenser. *A View of the Present State of Ireland*. 1596. Ed. W.L. Renwick. Oxford: Clarendon, 1970. 3.

[20]   Ibid. 14.

[21]   Ibid. 18.

[22]   Ibid. 823.

[23]   Ibid. 3.

[24]   John Derricke. *The Images of Ireland*. London, 1581: 'Lo lo I see, in Mowers crewel hande,/A fearful Sithe, which doeth prognosticate,/Both here and there, throughout this Irish lande/That growth of things, are at their ripened state/Whiche must be cropt, by Sithe of dismall fate.'

[25]   Spenser. *View*. 95.

exclusive. But by literally erasing Irish space—its land, its topography, and thus its culture—Spenser/England can then create a chorography that is inscribed with English identity. The problem that Spenser and other colonial servants do not fully recognize is the consequence of a blurred identity that would result from hegemony and in our specific argument here, through the manipulation of chorography (and I include all ideological tools that construct chorography). Significant to the imperialists, the imposed enclosure represents a territorial barrier between other colonizing forces such as Spain and France.

We must also note that Spenser's plan for Irish erasure directly attacks the Old English; for the 'corrupt' components of the land allude to those who have been assimilated into the Irish culture and have thus far prohibited a policy of radical colonization to take place in Ireland. *A View of the Present State of Ireland* demonstrates that the only way Ireland will overcome its present condition and become profitable for the crown is through this type of policy. I propose that what really bothered Spenser and his supporters was the fact that England, via the Old English, was already assimilated by the Irish through intermarriage, reproduction, traditions, customs, and language. Consider the various descriptions from *View* that support my assertion here: Eudoxus inquires, 'is it possible that an Englishman brought up naturally in such sweet civility as England affords could find such liking in that barbarous nation?',[26] and later observes 'how quickly doth that country alter men's natures!'[27] Eudoxus serves as the mouthpiece for Spenser and other New English who display anxiety over this assimilation. These questions serve to reveal that, regardless of how uncivil and base the colonizing body of England finds the Irish countryside, English have, in fact, relocated and *by their own choosing* have assimilated identities and cultures therein.

I incorporate a quote in my title to Chapter 3 that is not from the Elizabethan period;[28] rather, it comes from Irish playwright Brian Friel's *Translations*—a drama set during the Ordnance Survey[29] in Ireland in 1833. The ramifications of this English venture would not preclude the Anglicizing of Irish place-names and the literal/physical erosion of Irish culture. While Spenser's text was published some 237 years before the Ordnance Survey and Friel's play 147 years after that, we can see that hegemonic practices of the Elizabethans did not merely stop at the end of Elizabeth's or even James's reign. Rather, the erosion of Irish geographic space can still be felt in contemporary chorographies of that nation. In addition, although maps of land/space have been used as political tools, it has been argued that they are ideologically neutral.[30] 'Chorography,' 'surveys,' and 'descriptions' are not

---

[26] Ibid. 48.

[27] Ibid. 151.

[28] 'Something is being eroded.'

[29] The Ordnance Survey largely was responsible for anglicizing Irish place-names and the subsequent deculturation. For further reading, see Andrews, *Shapes of Ireland.* 20–23 and 277–309.

[30] Helgerson. *Forms of Nationhood.* 114.

necessarily so. Spenser's *A View of the Present State of Ireland*, therefore, offers the ultimate chorography of a space ripe for colonization. In reading this dialogue, we can recognize the skewed process whereby the subjection of the Other—as constructed in Elizabethan England—continues to complicate a national identity that remains blurred.

Shakespeare's Richard: or, a View of the Present State of England

While Spenser's contemporaries writing on Ireland and its people echo the poet's obtrusive stereotypes and concerns, Shakespeare grapples with these identical issues in his historical play *Richard II* and crucially chooses to show the hypocrisy implicit in these hegemonic assumptions. Whether or not Shakespeare read Spenser's propaganda before penning his play that focuses on the fall of one monarch and the rise of another remains a mystery; both texts were probably written in 1595 or shortly thereafter. But one thing is certain—the allusions which emblematize John of Gaunt's[31] nostalgic speech as he approaches death's door castigate Spenser's prose on Ireland. In addition, the issues of a diseased state, the dual agendas of the Old and New English, the allegorical references to the Garden of Eden, the importance of Ireland as an individual nation and the topographical polemics of land are addressed in both texts. However, the subtext exposes divergent agendas of these Elizabethan writers.

Although Spenser's *View* elucidates how literature can construct a map of authority, Shakespeare conversely shows the ramifications of such an attempt. Gaunt's 'scept'red isle' speech, like the St Crispian's Day speech in *Henry V*, remains one of the most quoted passages in Shakespearean drama and specifically serves as a wake-up call to Richard, who is on the verge of being deposed by Bolingbroke. Gaunt, Shakespeare's embodiment of the Old English faction, begins by talking of the past glories of the kingdom, and compares England to 'a seat of Mars,' 'demi-paradise,' and 'other Eden.' As Michael Neill elucidates, 'Gaunt's lyricism can be seen to expose other contradictions in the construction of English nationhood ... it is not "Britain" but "England" that is the subject of his panegyric.'[32] His visionary remarks soon shift focus and Gaunt cautions, 'This land of such dear souls, this dear dear land,/Dear for her reputations through the world,/Is now leas'd out—I die pronouncing it—/Like to a tenement or pelting farm' (II.i.57–60). While England is at first related to a celestial being, the end result is an Edenic—and thus, earthly—

---

[31]   John of Gaunt, Duke of Lancaster, was Richard II's uncle. Peter Saccio remarks that 'Shakespeare makes of this enormously powerful and wealthy man a patriotic and patriarchal figure of great probity and dignity ... the playwright departs from Holinshed, who, with far greater historical accuracy, depicts Gaunt as a contentious and ambitious baron.' *Shakespeare's English Kings: History, Chronicle, and Drama*. Oxford: Oxford UP, 1977. 20.

[32]   See his brilliant study, 'Broken English and Broken Irish: Nation, Language, and the Optic of Power in Shakespeare's Histories.' *Shakespeare Quarterly* 45.1 (1994): 14.

condition. In the descending order of things, Shakespeare portrays England as merely a territory that remains susceptible to mismanagement. Furthermore, Gaunt directly ridicules Richard and traces the demise of his power in the realm:

> Why cousin, wert thou regent of the world,
> It were a shame to let this land by lease;
> But for thy world enjoying but this land,
> Is it not more than shame to shame it so?
> Landlord of England art thou now, not king. (II.i.109–13)

In an interesting correlation with Spenser's text, we may examine the following statement regarding Irish 'tenements' by Eudoxus: 'it is a great willfulness in any such landlord, to refuse to make any longer farms unto their tenants, as may besides the general good of the realm, be also greatly for their own profit and avail.'[33] While Spenser focuses on the profits extracted by landlords of the Irish and the ruling order, thus negating the Irish people's capability to 'farm' their own territory, Shakespeare attaches negative connotations to Gaunt's indictment of the king as nothing more than a 'landlord.' As a result, Gaunt's speech actually presages the nation's faltering under the poor direction of Richard.

Clearly, geographical space appears to be important in defining the nation as its own individualized entity throughout the play. This is echoed by the Gardener's reference to England as a 'sea-walled garden' (III.iv.43) in *Richard II*. Similarly, Spenser also addresses the issue of space; but he does so in his description of Ireland as 'thus enclosed and well fenced' (83) in *A View*. This, in turn, emphasizes the colonizer's discreteness and at the same time serves as a form of trade protectionism that only fosters cultural and social fragmentation.

Also, we can identify a link here between Spenser's depiction of Ireland and Gaunt's pronouncement of England as they typify the Garden of Eden. While garden imagery in Shakespeare's play is plentiful, the quintessential segment of *Richard II* in relation to Eden appears in III. iv., where the anxious Queen Isabel's discourse with the gardeners foreshadows the king's fall from grace. With a call for order in England, the gardener beckons

> Go thou, like an executioner
> Cut off heads of [too] fast growing sprays,
> That look to lofty in our commonwealth:
> All must be even in our government.
> You thus employed, I will go root away
> The noisome weeds which without profit suck
> The soil's fertility from wholesome flowers. (33–9)

A balance at court is sorely lacking, and this recalls our previous investigation of the call for reform in Spenser's *View* as both writers inscribe their respective

---

[33]   Spenser. *View*. 82–3.

gardens with metaphors of unkempt plots of land. In Shakespeare's passage, the language suggests a pro-active position. Instead of encouraging a program of dispossession, however, Shakespeare's gardener intimates that only the 'noisome weeds'—Richard's flatterers—be rooted out in order to create a more fertile nation.

The first man describes Richard's forsaken kingdom as long past the stage of cure for its present disease. Here Shakespeare uses language similar Spenser's to communicate the chaotic state of Richard's realm:

When our sea-walled garden, the whole land,
is full of weeds, her fairest flowers chok'd up,
Her fruit trees all unprun'd, her hedges ruin'd,
Her knots disordered, and her wholesome herbs
Swarming with caterpillars? (43–7)

Operating as a binary correlative to Spenser's discourse, Shakespeare indicts *England* as a wasteland in need of redress. The caterpillars that invade the garden—Bushy, Bagot and Green—represent the serpent in the Adam and Eve narrative. Because of their superfluous intentions manifested through ill-counsel and superficial flattery, Richard loses the focus of his responsibilities as monarch. In turn, he forfeits his land and compromises his constituents, as prophesied by the gardener: 'I, what a pity is it/That he had not so trimm'd and dress'd his land/As we this garden!' (55–7). While the link with the garden motif in Spenser's *View* is more subtle and achieves different ends, Andrew Hadfield makes a connection between the 'lapse' that Spenser is afraid of and the 'naked savages' which he describes in *View*.[34] These naked inhabitants, signifying the Other in relation to their more civilized English counterparts, are thus likened to Adam and Eve in the post-lapserian world, and therefore England is compared with a Garden of Eden, as a lapsed nation in need of redemption. Herein lies another example of Shakespeare's clever manipulation of identical rhetoric; for he uses the gardening images as a representation of his internalist policy. Where Spenser's Edenic imagery attends to untamed Ireland, Shakespeare's is concerned with reform within England.

Another similarity between *A View of the Present State of Ireland* and *Richard II* can be seen in the depiction of Gaunt. He represents the old chivalric code at the dawning of a new era of dominance for England. This contrast parallels Spenser's depiction of the Old/New English dichotomy in Ireland. Initially, Eudoxus attacks the Old English because of their tendency to 'lean to their old customs and Brehon laws,'[35] and in a similar fashion, the impotent Richard mocks his honorable uncle as

---

[34] In '"The Naked and the Dead": Elizabethan Perceptions of Ireland.' *Travel and Drama in Shakespeare's Time*. Ed. Jean Pierre Maquerlot and Michele Willems. Cambridge: Cambridge UP, 1996.
[35] Spenser. *View*. 10

'Old John of Gaunt' (I.i.1) and 'aged Gaunt' (II.i.72).[36] The old ways are no longer fashionable, especially if a program of change is to occur.

In *View*, Irenius reveals 'it is the manner of all barbarous nations to be very superstitious and diligent observers of old customs and antiquities which they receive by continual tradition from their parents, by recording of their bards and chronicles in their songs, and by daily use and ensample of their elders.'[37] Irenius, like Richard, does not recognize the value of deep-rooted tradition embedded in a nation. And Gaunt is not the only character in Shakespeare's plot to appreciate the old order; for the Duchess of Gloucester asks 'old Gaunt,' 'Alack, and what shall good old York there see/But empty lodgings and unfurnish'd walls,/Unpeopled offices, untrodden stones?' (I.ii.679). By manipulating the identical metaphors of the rank, unweeded garden, Shakespeare critiques those involved in the domination and dispossession of Ireland.

Even subtextually, Ireland is important in Richard's policy, for his expedition there was a major event; it would be 290 years before another English monarch would visit.[38] Ireland is mentioned directly in *Richard II*, for the king is concerned with getting money and 'The lining of his coffers' (I.iv.61) with profits from his uncle's (John of Gaunt's) estate in order to engage in Irish wars. In *Richard II* Ireland 'serves as a convenient peripheral vehicle for maneuverings within the realm of England itself ... in Richard's case, the appropriation of Gaunt's resources.'[39] The inept monarch reveals his intent:

> Now for our Irish warres,
> We must supplant those rough rug-headed Kernes,
> Which live like venom where no venom else
> But only they have privilege to live.
> And, for these great affairs do ask some charge,
> Towards our assistance, we do seize to us
> The plate, coin, revenues, and moveables
> Whereof our uncle Gaunt did stand possess'd. (II.i.155–62)

Here Shakespeare's Richard mirrors Spenser's Elizabeth in *View*: 'I doubt not but if the Queen's coffers be not so well stored (which we are not to look into) but

---

[36]   As David Cairns and Shaun Richards assert, 'The New English argued that the culture of the Irish had led to the degeneration of those exposed to it—a threat exemplified for Spenser, amongst others, by the "Irish" traits, such as language and customs, displayed by the Old English who had intermarried freely with the Native Irish and so ceased, in New English eyes to be really English.' *Writing Ireland: Colonialism, Nationalism, and Culture.* Manchester: Manchester UP, 1988. 5.

[37]   Spenser. *View*. 60.

[38]   Sir D. Plunket Barton. *Links Between Ireland and Shakespeare.* Dublin: Maunsel and Co., 1919. 89.

[39]   Andrew Murphy. 'Shakespeare's Irish History.' *Literature and History* 5 (1996): 456.

that the whole realm, which now (as things are used) do feel a continual burden of that wretched realm hanging upon their backs' (96). Given Spenser's contention and the historical implications of Elizabeth's expenditures in Ireland,[40] we may deduce that Shakespeare's Richard is actually a construction of Elizabeth. Through the subtext of *Richard II*, Shakespeare not only usurps the language of the typical colonial servant (Spenser) and uses it to expose the fallacies in his campaign of total assimilation; but the playwright also extends an arm of caution to a monarch who, if given the right circumstances, may follow the disparaging comments of the Elizabethan propagandists, the New English, and adopt a policy of deterritorialization in Ireland.

Resistance is Futile: Assimilation and the Celtic Other in *Henry V*

Shakespeare once again plies the history play genre in 1599 through an examination of the cause/effect of colonial discourse in *Henry V*, the final component of the *Henriad*. In particular, Shakespeare establishes the Subject/Object relationship under the strains of imperialism and raises profound questions regarding national identity and the fact of 'Englishness.' King Henry V was hailed as 'the most successful incarnation of English nationalism,'[41] and during his nine-and-a-half year reign, there was no threat of civil strife posed against him. However, as Shakespeare articulates in the history play, there exists evidence of international conflict which cannot be overlooked. As I have argued, English national identity, as portrayed poignantly through English history, is based upon domination of the Other. In his famous history play *Henry V*, Shakespeare renders rival Western European nations as the Other and exposes how not only the Third World countries frequently cited by postcolonial critics—but any political entity—can be rendered into the Other to suit the purpose of some primary country's national identity. In three separate situations in the text, he illustrates the concept of England's relation to the oppressed; first, in terms of another imperial force (France), second, through characters from colonized Western diasporic communities (Ireland, Scotland, and Wales) who serve under Henry, and finally, through the usurpation of the female (Katherine) who is marginalized as a mere commodity as she is exchanged between her regal French father and the victorious Hal.

If we recall Bolingbroke's deathbed speech in *2 Henry IV* to his heir apparent—'Therefore, my Harry,/Be it thy course to busy giddy minds/ With foreign quarrels' (IV.v.212–14)—it is not surprising that Henry follows his father's advice. Instigated

---

[40]   As Phyllis Rackin ascertains: 'Richard's outrageous fiscal exactions as well as his confiscation of Gaunt's escape are motivated by his need for money for Irish wars, the same need that constituted Queen Elizabeth's major financial burden in the late 1590s.' *Stages of History: Shakespeare's English Chronicles*. Ithaca, NY: Cornell UP. 100.

[41]   Annabel Patterson. *Reading Holinshed's* Chronicles. Chicago: University of Chicago Press. 131.

by the Archbishop of Canterbury and the Bishop of Ely, Henry wants to ensure (primarily to gain public support) that his endeavors in France are justified considering the proclamation that 'No woman shall succeed in Salique land' (I.ii.39). However, Canterbury believes that France 'would hold up this Salique law/To bar your highness claiming from the female' (I.ii.92).[42] Encouraged by his counselors, despite the bloody prospects[43] that battle will yield for both 'mighty kingdoms,' Henry proceeds to threaten the French king, and this particular scene ends with his patriotic creed: 'The signs of war advance! No King of England, if not King of France!' (II.ii.192–3). The king's thirst for power over his imperial neighbor is carried to an extreme, for despite all of the prayers he invokes and his double-talk concerning mercy, Henry desires political hegemony over a territory—in this case, France.

We can extrapolate historical relevance to Henry V here by assessing the correspondence between Elizabeth and Spanish Captain Diego Ortiz de Urizar, whose intentions for Ireland's allegiance were motivated primarily by its convenient proximity to England. Spain's designs on Ireland for 'defence of the Catholic faith,' 'eradication of heresy,' and 'help sent to an oppressed country,' 'were all expressions that hid under a more sordid and materialistic end: the capture of England.'[44] But two specific segments of this important political correspondence yield reference to Shakespeare's *Henry V*. The first is Urizar's proclamation, 'Quien Inglaterra quiere conquistar por Irlanda ha de comenzar'—which translates from Spanish to English as 'He who wants to capture England must begin his task in Ireland.'[45] Quite conceivably, Shakespeare manipulates this advice and plants it in the mouth of the bishop's proclamation to Henry with regard to Scotland.[46] The second allusion occurs in a letter to Philip II from the Queen dated March 1571, where Elizabeth articulates her position that Ireland belongs to England: 'The realm our parents and grandparents possessed.'[47] This notation bears similarity to Henry's claim on the French throne, and reveals that Shakespeare constructs King Henry in the form of Elizabeth and France as Ireland.

The French, possessing a counter-hegemonic mindset, do not realize the seriousness of the English king's gestures, for the young Dolphin assures his father that Hal is no threat to their mighty army, and with an air of dismissal assures 'she

---

42 Andrew Murphy posits that 'the purpose of Salike Law (in Canterbury's historicist view) is to prevent the very assimilation of the colonizer by the colonized (through intermarriage) that Spenser decries in *A View*.' *But the Irish Sea Betwixt Us: Ireland, Colonialism, and Renaissance Literature*. Lexington: UP of Kentucky. 112.

43 Henry says, 'Therefore take heed how you impawn our person,/How you awake our sleeping sword of war—/ ... For never two kingdoms did contend/ Without much fall of blood' (I.ii.21–2, 24–5).

44 Tazón-Salces. 'Politics, Literature and Colonization.' 189.

45 Ibid.

46 Ely advises King Henry, 'If that you will France win, / Then with Scotland first begin' (I.ii.167–8). These lines ring curiously close to Urizar's remark to Elizabeth.

47 Tazón-Salces. 'Politics, Literature and Colonization.' 190.

is so idly king'd,/Her sceptre so fantastically borne,/By a vain, giddy, shallow, humorous youth,/That fear attends her not' (II.iv.26–9). Shakespeare uses this context to depict France's attempt to create an-Other entity for the English by highlighting the monarch's weakness and feminization of the land. Interestingly, however, the feminization of the land may relate specifically to Elizabeth; certainly, the act of deterritorialization for imperial purposes counted on envisioning the land in question as a female in order to highlight its weakness. 'Feminized, the land becomes a fitting object for male desire and appropriation.'[48] Evidence shows that during Elizabeth's reign, negative propaganda infiltrated England and her territories that play on her vulnerability because of her sex,[49] and the queen's 'bodily borders served as a metonymy for the geographical and political borders of her island nation.'[50] But even more interesting is the fact that France is also feminized, for inevitably Katherine serves as the bargaining piece between her father and Henry, and she is commodified as a mode of reproduction. Furthermore, a discussion of rights of women and property are inserted at the onset of the play when Henry and his advisors invoke Salique Law to solidify his rights to the French throne. Finally, the references to raping the land once again allude to the feminization of France; in III.iii we hear the 'godly king' mention rape three times in his threatening speech at Harfleur, for he proclaims that his military/political campaign will be like a soldier 'mowing like grass/Your fresh fair virgins' (III.iii.13–14) and his lusty men 'with foul hand/ '[Defile] the locks of your shrilling daughters' (34–5). Through this colonizing discourse, Shakespeare reveals to the audience that Henry has one purpose concerning his affairs in France, and he will stop at nothing—even it requires raping and pillaging innocent bystanders—to usurp the French throne and assimilate the kingdoms.

Shakespeare filters in the scenes from the French camp in order to both mock and stereotype the French army and illustrate that, to a large extent, the French leaders simply do not take England seriously. Henry's soldiers are easily dismissed as a 'sick and famish'd' (III.v.57) lot and 'a barbarous people' (III.v.4) who will not pose a serious threat to them.[51] This crucial factor directly leads to the downfall of the French at the Battle of Agincourt and, more importantly, articulates Shakespeare's manipulation of Spenser's metaphors of weakness and impotence which function

---

[48]   Helgerson. *Forms of Nationhood.* 124.

[49]   As Christopher Highley observes, 'Elizabeth ... acted as surrogate mother ... to her Irish subjects by fostering the sons of Irish nobility at the English court. 'The Royal Image in Elizabethan Ireland.' According to the New English author Barnabe Rich, the queen was ever 'a loving nurse, nay rather a kinde mother, that did still carke and care for [her Irish subjects], with such compassionate love and kindness'. *A New Description of Ireland.* 67. But Rich's depiction speaks for other members of the New English who sought to appropriate an image of weakness for the queen because of what they saw as softness towards the Irish people.

[50]   Highley. 'The Royal Image in Elizabethan Ireland.' 69.

[51]   Andrew Murphy makes an interesting connection between France's disgust for the 'bastard Normans' and Edmund Spenser's derision for the Old English. *But the Irish Sea Betwixt Us.*112.

in *A View of the Present State of Ireland* by conjuring negative attitudes about the Irish.

The overconfidence which exudes from French characters such as the Dolphin, Constable, and King soon wanes, for eventually the fear of assimilation surfaces in the play as a very realistic threat for them. This concept is best exemplified in III. v.28–31:

> By faith and honor,
> Our madams mock at us, and plainly say
> Our mettle is bred out, and they will give
> Their bodies to the lust of English youth
> To new-store France with bastard warriors.

The Dolphin articulates what lies in the minds of many French, and in fact Henry's usurpation of the French princess immediately following the English victory at Agincourt serves as a fulfillment of this prophecy. The French treat the English as the Other in the same way that the marginalized representatives in Hal's army remain in the peripheral realm of the Subject/Object relationship. But what may be deemed more problematic is the evidence of a chaotic disposition in the defeated country:

> Should not in this best garden of the world,
> Our fertile France, put up her lovely visage?
> Alas, she hath from France too long been chas'd,
> And all her husbandry doth lie on heaps,
> Corrupting in it own fertility.
> Her vine, the merry cheerer of the heart,
> Unpruned dies; her hedges even-pleach'd
> Like prisoners wildly overgrown with hair,
> Put forth disorder'd twigs ... (V.2.36–44)

The status of France which Burgundy describes once again evokes images of Spenser's Ireland as wasteland in the play and England as Richard's garden. Both texts describe the nations in question as 'unpruned' and desolate lands; and perhaps Shakespeare's portrait of France at the close of the *Henriad* serves as a reminder of the state of Elizabethan England at the commencement of this historical chronicle; this is also indicative of all nations that have, like Ireland, become subjected to imperial hegemony. The assimilative cycle which King Richard embarks on unsuccessfully in *Richard II* is now complete as the marriage of Katherine and Henry represents the culmination of England's imperial process. And yet Shakespeare assesses the blurring of identity once again as represented through fears of a bastardized French landscape.

For this cultural hybridization of nations to occur, sexual union must be addressed as it functions in the colonizer's scheme. Henry's right to the throne could not be manifested simply through his victory on the battlefield, for he must turn to 'a woman—a *French* woman'—in order to legitimize his rule in France.[52] Katherine, daughter of the French king, serves as a pawn between the two opposing hegemonies, for before a treaty is signed, Henry instructs everyone to 'leave our cousin Katherine here with us/She is our capital demand' (V.ii.96–7). In a scene that appears comical on the stage but contains serious implications, Henry attempts to win the love of the French princess. While Katherine cannot speak English, Henry uses the discourse of the colonizer to woo her. Although he makes an initial attempt to speak to her in French, he insists on communicating with her in his native tongue. Also, Henry 'anglicizes' her name by calling her 'Kate.' Katherine wonders, 'Is it possible dat I should love de enemie of France?' (V.ii.169–70). Henry, gifted with eloquent rhetoric, responds,

> No, it is not possible you should love the
> enemy of France, Kate; but in loving me, you should
> love the friend of France; for I love France so well that
> I will not part with a village of it; I will have it all
> mine. And, Kate, when France is mine and I am yours,
> then yours is France and you are mine. (V.171–6)

Hardly considered a romantic pursuit, Henry's master plan revolves around possession—of land, of villages, of people. Pursuing his itinerary further, he remarks that Katherine 'must therefore needs prove a good soldier-breeder' (V.ii.205–6) and inquires, 'Shall not thou and I, between Saint Denis and Saint George, compound a boy, half French, half English, that shall go to Constantinople and take the Turk by the beard?' (V.ii.206–9). The French leaders' earlier fears that France would be bastardized by English warriors appear imminent: while Shakespeare raises the awareness of the outcome of blurred national identities at the same time, he exposes a campaign of colonization in the East.

As the play draws to a close, Henry informs Katherine, 'England is thine, Ireland is thine, France is thine, and *Henry Plantaginet* is thine' (V.ii.239–40). Henry's discourse signifies a continuum of colonization and oppression that is in store for England's monarchy. Not only does Shakespeare illustrate the young monarch's colonizing of young Katherine—who is therefore assimilated into *English* history—but he also shows how Henry's imperial campaign will persist and penetrate other nations and cultures. The penultimate effect of Henry's union with the French princess marks a loss of identity as a result of the breeding that the Dolphin fears earlier in the play and the propagation that Henry hopes for with Katherine. While this might be Henry's idea of 'wooing,' this disingenuous discourse intends to promote and reinforce the King's agenda of complete assimilation, of an imperialistic hybridity; and although the play ends with a royal wedding, no blissful union of nations or identities actually occurs. In fact, the Epilogue reveals that with the untimely death of the King, his young, inexperienced son ascends to the throne and 'lost France,

---

[52]   Phyllis Rackin. *Stages of History*. 167.

and made his England bleed' (12). Even more revealing are the preceding lines which describe Henry V's reign: 'Fortune made his sword;/By which the world's best garden he achieved,/And of it left his son imperial lord' (6–8). By including this particular epilogue, Shakespeare further exposes the pitfalls of unwarranted colonial enterprise.

With the inclusion of the captains' scene in Act III, Shakespeare affords the audience an even more striking and relevant vehicle through which assimilation is manifested. Stephen Greenblatt posits that this final component of the *Henriad* 'insists that we have all along been both colonizer and colonized, king and subject.'[53] Also,

> By yoking together diverse peoples—represented in the play by the Welshman Fluellen, the Irishman Macmorris, and the Scotsman Jamy, who fight at Agincourt alongside the loyal Englishmen—Hal symbolically tames the last wild areas in the British Isles, areas that in the sixteenth century represented, far more powerfully than any New World people, the doomed outposts of a vanishing tribalism.[54]

Yet while these characters may be, as Greenblatt interjects, 'yoked together,' they *do* retain their distinctive identities relative to their nations. For example, the characters speak in different dialects that are noticeably distinct from each other and they talk openly about their individual nation(s).

The Irishman Macmorris, the Welshman Fluellen, and the Scotsman Jamy represent the Celtic Other who serve under the king. Although the captains in Act III tease each other about their respective regional dialects and customs, they appear unified under Henry.[55] However, evidence of dissension exists among these countries, as witnessed in Fluellen's taunting of Macmorris and the insertion of the leek segment involving Pistol and the Welshman. Certain identities seem to be granted a more favored nation status in the play. In particular, we can detect a strong sense of Welshness,[56] significant perhaps to Elizabeth's Tudor ancestry, hearkening back to Henry VII. One of the key indicators of this ideological preference occurs at the beginning of the final Act, where Fluellen confronts Pistol about the leeks. Gower, whose name is Welsh, reprimands 'Ancient Pistol':

---

[53]   Stephen Greenblatt. 'Invisible Bullets: Renaissance Authority and its Subversion, *Henry IV* and *Henry V.' Political Shakespeare: Essays in Cultural Materialism*. Ed. Jonathan Dollimore and Alan Sinfield. 2nd ed. Manchester: Manchester UP, 1994. 42.

[54]   Ibid.

[55]   Saccio. *Shakespeare's English Kings*. 70.

[56]   For an in-depth discussion of this issue, see Patricia Parker's 'Uncertain unions: Welsh leeks in *Henry V.' British Identities and English Renaissance Literature*. Ed. David J. Baker and Willy Maley. Cambridge: Cambridge UP, 2002. 81–100.

You thought, because he could not speak
English in the native garb, he could not therefore
handle an English cudgel. You find it otherwise, and
henceforth let a Welsh correction teach you a good
English condition. (V.i.75–9)

Gower, who remains separate from the bantering between the nations throughout the play, suddenly takes a stab at Pistol, and a definite bias can be identified in the play. Here exists an example of the preeminence given to the Welsh soldiers; for Shakespeare appears to reject a general vision of unity under the direction of Henry.

Ironically, Scotland remains, for the most part, nonconfrontational and largely subdued. For example, when the Irish Captain Macmorris[57] is commended by Gower, Fluellen[58] states, 'By Chesu, he is an ass, as in the world; I will/ verify as much in his beard. He has no more directions/in the true disciplines of the wars, look you, of the Roman disciplines, than is a puppy dog' (III.i.70–73). But Jamy quickly interjects, 'He is a falorous man.' Scotland, via Jamy, acts here as an intermediary and is a far cry from Ely's stereotype of England's northern neighbor as a 'weasel.' In fact, Henry wonders about the threat of 'the Scot,/Who hath been still a giddy neighbor to us' (I.ii.144–5) while England ponders military maneuvers in France.

It is also noteworthy to remind the reader that the unsuspecting French Dolphin refers to Henry as 'giddy' (II.iv.28). 'Threat is defused in the homely familiarity of the twin reassurance of "giddiness" and "neighborhood", terms which assimilate the Scots within the known and accepted rather than demonizing them or othering them.'[59] Shakespeare's depiction of Jamy as a representative of the Scottish culture appears to dismiss Ely's earlier prodding to Henry, where he recalls the old saying,

---

[57]   Shakespeare's Macmorris has been classified as the first Irish character to appear on the English stage. Concerning the diverse nationalities in the last play in the *Henriad*, Joan Rees remarks that in 'Shakespeare's Welshmen,' 'Political considerations may have inhibited Shakespeare from making more than he did of Macmorris and Jamy in *Henry V*, but it was evidently not unfamiliarity with the accents that held him back. Gary Taylor, annotating the Scots, Irish and Welsh voices, comments that stage Scotsmen appear from at latest, 1577, but that MacMorris may be the first Elizabethan stage Irishman'. 'Shakespeare's Welshmen.' *Literature and Nationalism*. Ed. Vincent Newey and Ann Thompson. Liverpool: Liverpool UP, 1991. 37.

[58]   For a detailed account of the role of Fluellen in *Henry V*, see Rees, 'Shakespeare's Welshmen.'

[59]   Lisa Hopkins. 'Neighbourhood in *Henry V*.' *Shakespeare and Ireland: History, Politics, Culture*. Ed. Mark Thornton Burnett and Ramona Wray. New York: St Martin's, 1997. 10.

If that you will France win,
Then with Scotland first begin.'
For once the eagle (England) being in prey,
To her unguarded nest the weasel (Scotland)
Comes sneaking, and so sucks her princely eggs,
Playing the mouse in absence of the cat,
To 'tame and havoc more than she can eat. (I.ii.167–73)

Rehashing the unrest in England when the Scottish, led by William Wallace, ransacked their country while the King, Edward Longshanks, was fighting elsewhere, Ely—serving to promulgate hegemonic principles at court—cautions Henry to take heed against his colonized neighbors. But even the hot-tempered Fluellen commends his Scottish counterpart: 'By Chesu, he will maintain his argument as well as any military man in the world, in the disciplines of the pristine wars of the Romans' (III. i.79–82).

Considering the historical implications in Elizabethan England, Joan Rees offers,

> The presence of Irish and Scots captains in Henry's army speaks similarly for a united kingdom, but union with Scotland is still to come and, in 1599, there was only an in-the-end-unfulfilled hope that Ireland might be pacified: tactfully Shakespeare does not ask too much of his Irishman and Scotsman but puts the weight of his theme of unification on Fluellen. The theme is a serious one and Shakespeare is at pains to acknowledge and give honourable notice to Welsh qualities.[60]

While Rees's articulation of the tenuous relationship between England, Scotland and Ireland is applicable here—as is the Welsh issue, given Henry's (and Elizabeth I's) ancestral Welsh heritage—Shakespeare places great importance on the other captains. Also, by downplaying the tenuous relationship between Scotland and England and highlighting the bond between Welsh and English, Shakespeare calls the audience to focus on the positioning of the Irish.

It might be argued that Shakespeare portrays Henry, to a small extent,[61] as a monarch concerned with the common man, for the Chorus mentions his mixing with the lowbrow soldiers who feel 'A little touch of Harry in the night.' Also, after hearing the concerns of the peasant soldiers who are ill and close to starvation, Henry gives

---

[60] Rees. 'Shakespeare's Welshmen.' 29.

[61] Although the Chorus paints the English monarch as a friend of the common man, Shakespeare reveals Henry's duplicitous nature in IV.viii through his inquiry, 'Where is the number of our English dead?' (102). Upon receiving the list, he remarks, 'Edward the Duke of York, the Earl of Suffolk,/Sir Richard Ketly, Davy Gam, esquire;/None else of name; and of all other men/But five and twenty' (103–6).

what has become one of the most popular discourses in Shakespearean drama[62]—the St Crispin's Day speech:

> We few, we happy few, we band of brothers;
> For he to-day that sheds his blood with me
> Shall be my brother; be he ne'er so vile,
> This day shall gentle his condition;
> And gentlemen in England, now a-bed,
> Shall think themselves accurs'd they were not here;
> And hold their manhoods cheap whiles any speaks
> That fought with us upon Saint Crispin's day. (IV.iii.60–67)

It strikes a curious chord, though, that the common soldiers in this play, as opposed to the officers, are *English* only, and we could argue that his target is the English gentry ('gentlemen in England, now a-bed'); therefore, this speech becomes a class issue, too, in addition to the already pervasive political identity matter. Perhaps Henry's interaction with the other nationalities in the English camp provides clearer light regarding the monarch's unifactory policies. For example, in IV.i.51 Henry declares 'I am a Welshman'; and when queried about his familiarity with the Welsh Fluellen, he responds, 'And his kinsman too' (59). What follows is a sentimental discourse between Henry and Fluellen based on the leek, a national symbol of Wales.

> *Fluellen*: Your grandfather of famous memory, an't
>   please your Majesty, and your great-uncle
>   Edward the
>   Plack Prince of Wales, as I have read in the chronicles,
>   fought a most prave pattle here in France.
> *Henry*: They did, Fluellen. (IV.vii.92–6)

Here, Shakespeare establishes the historical connection between Henry and Wales by divulging his Welsh ancestry. Fluellen then continues to reiterate the monarch's Welshness in an attempt to move from the Subject of the Object position in the scheme of the colonial Other:

---

[62]   Because of the patriotic reaction to this speech, Winston Churchill asked Laurence Olivier to make a *Henry V* film in order to boost morale in England following World War II.

Fluellen: All the water in Wye cannot wash your
Majesty's Welsh plood out of your pody, I can tell you
that. God pless it, and preserve it, as long as it pleases
his Grace, and his Majesty too!
Henry: Thanks, good my [countryman].
Fluellen: By Jeshu, I am your Majesty's countryman,
I care not who know it. I will confess it to all the world. (IV.vii.106–13)

With the repetition of 'countryman,' and in particular Fluellen's act of identification with the king, Shakespeare again exposes the blurred nationalities perpetuated throughout the play. When appropriate among his soldiers, Henry can alter his national identity and declare himself a Welshman; but as we see throughout the rest of the text, the monarch aligns himself with the English gentry.

It is clear from this passage that Fluellen, representative of the Welsh constituency, is privileged over the Other national constituencies. Furthermore, the Scottish captain Jamy appears to neutralize the other nationalities. What follows is a most impressive fight for victory in which the underdog wins, since England was so seriously outnumbered. Through these examples, we see that Henry's relation to England's troublesome colonies—Ireland, Scotland, and Wales—poses no inherent problem for the monarch on the battlefield, and his attempts to bond with the Others incites a sense of camaraderie amongst the unlikely group. However, the fact of identity remains under question despite the military success for England.

This complex issue concerning a unified national identity cannot be tied up neatly, and this is best illustrated through the pivotal passage which follows in III. ii.120–24:

Fluellen: Captain Macmorris, I think, look you, under
your correction, there is not many of your nation—
Macmorris: Of my nation? What ish my nation? Ish a
villain, and a basterd, and a knave, and a rascal.
What ish my nation? Who talks of my nation?

Quite clearly, cultural identity, separate from Englishness, remains blurred for the colonized. Perhaps Macmorris's statement, 'Ish a villain, and a basterd, and a knave, and a rascal' adheres to the stereotypes propagated by the colonizers who continually denigrate the Irish people. This portion of *Henry V* and especially the question 'What ish my nation?' continues to baffle scholars who insert a variety of interpretations which I will outline.

David Cairns and Shaun Richards refer to *Threshold of a Nation*, one of the earliest texts to address Ireland and national identity in relation to Macmorris. Following Philip Edwards argument, they claim:

Macmorris's outburst is a denial of such separate status, brought on by the sensed implication in the words of Fluellen, that while the Welsh may speak from within the united State, Macmorris is a member of a separate and therefore marginal group ... The process of self-fashioning required the continued presence of an 'other' so that the maintenance of subtle points of differentiation from the colonizer would continue to reproduce, not only the subordination of the colonized, but the superordination of the colonizer.[63]

While I agree with this assessment, the issue of the Other needs to be addressed to a larger extent; while the Irish captain undoubtedly represents a marginalized people wherein degrees of difference are manifested most obviously through his accent, we must also account for the marginality of the Scottish and even the Welsh. Certainly, there is a strong sense of Welsh culture inherent in the text, as embodied in Fluellen's interaction with Henry:

> *Fluellen*:   If your Majes-
> ties is rememb'red of it, the Welshmen did good
> service in a garden where leeks did grow, wearing leeks
> in their Monmouth caps, which, your Majesty
> know, to this hour is an honorable badge of the service;
> and I do believe your Majesty takes no scorn to wear
> the leek upon Saint Tavy's day.
> *King*:   I wear it for a memorable honor;
> For I am Welsh, you know, good countryman. (IV.vii.97–105)

Despite the link between regal leader and soldier, we cannot forget that Wales is colonized by England and the Welsh faced the same prospect of assimilation as the Others. But as mentioned earlier, the evidence suggests that the Welsh have less to worry about because they emphasize the connectivity in a way that suggests mutual cooperation rather than assimilation through political/cultural pressure. The fact that Henry addresses Fluellen as his 'countryman' speaks volumes to the audience as no other unification is attempted with any of the other nationalities. As Shakespeare portrays him, Henry remains the colonizer, a role he eases into and out of rather smoothly.

Interpretations of Macmorris's highly debated question abound. Philip Edwards offers an alternative reading of the discourse:

> The paraphrase should run something like this. 'What is this separate race you're implying by using the phrase "your nation"? Who are you, a Welshman, to talk of the Irish as though they were a separate nation from you? I belong in this family as much as you do.' This is the essence of it—indignation that a Welshman should think of Ireland as a separate nation from the great (British) nation to which the Welshman apparently thought he belonged.[64]

While his suggested rendering incorporates the discordant tonal quality of Shakespeare's Macmorris, Edwards is, in effect, posing the idea that Ireland (and Scotland and Wales, for that matter) is not a distinct, separate entity from England; and this is highly problematic. Andrew Murphy similarly asserts that Edwards

---

[63]   Cairns and Richards. *Writing Ireland*. 10.
[64]   Philip Edwards. *Threshold of a Nation*. Cambridge: Cambridge UP, 1979. 75–6.

'disregards the possibility that Irish's question may be just that—a genuine question: 'What ish my nation' … it is a blunt expression of this uncertainty, an interrogation of what constitutes the *Irish nation*.'[65] With the nebulous boundaries between nations, Murphy's assessment serves the reader well, and the critic takes this debate one step further by declaring 'if Irish's question can be related both to the condition of "Irishness" and to that ambiguous state at which distinctive national identities fail to be sustained, we should note that the question is also pertinent to the issue of the evocation of an *English* national identity.'[66] Enter the Welsh and Scottish captains into this equation, along with Henry's heritage and his vow to his French princess to be 'a soldier breeder,' and the idea of an English identity exists in a similar, indistinguishable space. According to James Shapiro, 'The desire on the part of the English to define themselves as different from, indeed free of, that which was Jewish, operated not on an individual level but on a national level as well.'[67] Shapiro's study can also be applied to the Irish and the other marginalized peoples who were associated with England in terms of the dispossession of a people and their land.

Andrew Hadfield offers another explication of Macmorris's Irish question which is worth mentioning:

> What is Macmorris asking here? Is he denying the efficacy of his Irishness and affirming a solidarity with the other Britons with whom he is fighting? Or is he anticipating an attack on his national identity and so preparing to defend the loyalty of the Irish to the English/ British crown? The text is enigmatic, confronting the audience with the problem rather than suggesting a solution.[68]

I agree with Hadfield's second position, for the Irish captain is prepared for an attack and the idea that Shakespeare poses the problem for the audience is paramount; for we must address the question of whether or not there would even be a solution to suggest. After four hundred years, the Irish question *still* remains unanswered in the United Kingdom. But the fact that Shakespeare includes this confrontational query in his text translates into the cultural consciousness of the late Renaissance.

More importantly, however, is the manifestation of this 'What ish my nation?'/Irish section in *Henry V*. First, consider the lines from the Act V prologue. Traditionally, the Irish rebellion reference is given to Essex for a conquest/tour through the isle in 1599. Regarding Hal's return to London and his subsequent 'uniting' of English loyalties, the chorus reveals 'now the general of our gracious empress,/As in good time he may, from Ireland coming,/Bringing rebellion broached on his sword'

---

65   Murphy. *But the Irish Sea Betwixt Us.* 118.
66   Ibid. 119.
67   James Shapiro. *Shakespeare and the Jews.* New York: Columbia UP, 1996. 42.
68   Andrew Hadfield. '"Hitherto she ne're could fancy him": Shakespeare's "British" Plays and the Exclusions of Ireland.' *Shakespeare and Ireland: History, Politics, Culture.* Ed. Mark Thornton Burnett and Ramona Wray. New York: St Martin's, 1997. 50.

(30–32). This reference to Shakespeare's contemporary Irish state seems pertinent to the condition of interpreting Macmorris's comments. With the argument that Shakespeare gives voice to the Irish margin, the placement of Macmorris's speech can (and is) certainly read as a criticism of Essex's/Elizabeth's/England's treatment of Ireland. Also note that where the chorus mentions the plebeians flocking to Caesar, Fluellen makes mention of the 'Roman wars' and, being Welsh, seems to accept these disciplines (which have conquered Ireland/the Roman Empire) as a definition of 'nation.' Fluellen's quarrel with Macmorris is that he is undisciplined and does not know therefore what his 'nation' is.

Macmorris clearly rejects Fluellen's definition, Shakespeare importantly allows him to be heard on stage, and the later reference in Act V by the chorus to the Irish rebellion therefore seems a reminder, if not criticism, that Ireland is not part of the English nation. In praising the 'Empress' Elizabeth, Shakespeare picks a flaw in the English armor as well as Elizabethan policy. Finally, it is important that Macmorris tells Fluellen, 'I do not know you so good a man as myself' (III.ii.32) and asserts his (and thus Ireland's) own sense of independence while biting Fluellen's definition of nation/Ireland.

The sense of 'Englishness,' then, concerning Shakespeare's *Henry V*, is based on a national identity associated with first, political force, as exemplified through the king's ravishing of France on her own land; second, through assimilation of the Other in an all-encompassing brand of Englishness—as elucidated through the loyalty of Macmorris, Fluellen and Jamy; and finally through the oppression of the female, as we see with the French princess Katherine, and her imposed identity as an English queen. Whereas England already has a colonial relationship with Ireland, so much so that Macmorris is conscripted into the army, France has not; therefore, through the feminization of the land and Henry's quest for assimilation and territory, France can be read as Ireland in Shakespeare's play.

Rather than justifying England's sense of nationalism, or applauding it, Shakespeare points us to the malignancy of colonization. As with *Richard II* and *A View of the Present State of Ireland*, Shakespeare indicts the Spenserian mindset for an imperialistic agenda that denigrates the objectified Irish as barbarians. Furthermore, while *Henry V* has been interpreted, misinterpreted, and reinterpreted as a godly, Christian king, the Stratfordian arguably portrays him as a double-talking, deceitful, hegemonic figure. Shakespeare's questioning and indictment of the Subject/Object relationships in *Henry V* demonstrate how the idea of an 'English' national identity surfaces as a facade.

In consideration of the mechanisms of the Subject/Object relationship in these texts, we must turn to Homi Bhabha,[69] who states that 'the representation of colonial authority depends less on a universal symbol of English identity than on its productivity as a sign of difference' (108). As long as the difference remains pronounced and the perpetuation of stereotypes remains visible—as exemplified from the colonial

---

[69]   Homi Bhabha. *The Location of Culture*. London: Routledge, 1994.

writings of Elizabethan England through those still penned today—subjectivity of the Other will continue to push them to ask the question, 'What ish my nation?'

Chapter 2

'Past and to Come Seems Best; Things Present Worse': Appropriations Of Shakespeare's *Henriad* in Modern Irish Drama

The contrary ideological positions held by Spenser and Shakespeare mark the latter as a subversive heterodox thinker on Irish issues which inevitably made his texts available to cultural appropriation by twentieth-century Irish dramatists. In the early 1900s, the Irish literati attempted to achieve an identity distinct from the discourses established by England. Interestingly, the dramatists were heavily influenced by the ways in which Shakespeare's plays constructed nationalism. These Irish playwrights raised Macmorris's inquiry regarding his nation and identity in their own texts. A chief area of contention concerned the representation of Irish characters on the English stage. The founders of the Abbey Theatre hoped to recuperate the stage Irishman to produce naturalistic portrayals of the Irish in Dublin. Despite the Abbey Board of Directors' commitment to an apolitical agenda, their efforts toward a legitimate Irish stage presence resulted in both the Playboy and Plough riots. These incidents culminated in the politicizing of the Irish stage and were largely based on linguistic misunderstanding and social class difference between the audience and characters.

In Ireland, the onset of the twentieth century marks an important era in terms of the nation's identity. Despite the literary achievements of the seventeenth, eighteenth, and nineteenth centuries,[1] it was not until the twentieth century that this colonized nation's cultural awareness blossomed and became inextricably linked with politics and art. Key events—including the 1916 Easter Rising, the Irish Civil War and the subsequent signing of the 1921 Treaty partitioning Northern Ireland from the remainder of the country—inflamed patriotism among the Irish.

It was against a blurred political landscape that this resurgent nationalistic view emerged and despite the heroism of statesmen such as Padraic Pearse, organizer

---

[1]   The problems of the Irish stage in the late eighteenth century are discussed in *An Answer to the Memoirs of Mrs. Billington*. London: 1792: 'The Irish theatre is supposed to be the hotbed for actors … In its present state, however, it can scarcely be placed in competition with the most insignificant of our provincial theatres, in point of acting.' 33–4.

of the Irish Citizen Army and primary artificer of the Easter Rising, and Michael Collins, who signed the Anglo-Irish Treaty in December 1921, this heightened awareness of an Irish identity was partially realized through the literary achievements promoted by the Irish National Theatre founded in 1899 and its offspring the Abbey Theatre launched five years later in Dublin. Well-respected literary figures such as Lady Augusta Gregory and William Butler Yeats devoted their energies to this new venture and afforded identity-conscious Irish playwrights a stage on which their socio-political views could be heard by the masses.

Those founders of the modern Irish stage wanted to steer away from any national type-casting with the Abbey. Because of its marginalized status, Ireland had long been deprived of her language, her identity, and a literature that could be singularly constituted as 'Irish.' A serious problem faced the 'truly native Irish writer of English: how can he render the speech of the Irish countryman without falling into the "bull-and-blunder" convention associated with Irish characters on the English stage from Shakespeare and Ben Jonson onwards?'[2] This challenge became clear to the Irish literati who entertained success in their homeland during the waning years of the nineteenth century, and specifically in the watershed year 1904. It was at this time that Yeats and Lady Gregory opened the doors of the Abbey Theatre with the help of Edward Martyn, George Moore, and the financial support of the Englishwoman Annie Horniman (whose main interest was Yeats and not the advancement of the literary revival in Ireland). They desired a more naturalistic depiction of the Irish that would eradicate the traditional characterizations of the nation as uncivil and drive the stereotype of the perpetual alcoholic fop from the twentieth-century stage.

Counter-Hegemony and the Abbey Theatre

The quest for individualism among the Irish precipitated a unified effort on the part of the predominant literary figures to draw national and cultural boundaries that were distinct from England. According to Brenna Katz Clarke,

> In November 1891, Charles Stewart Parnell, the disastrously compromised Home Rule leader of Ireland, died, and with him the political hopes of many young Irishmen. Many turned their energies from politics to literature and to the growing language revival movement. If Ireland could not achieve political separatism from England, at least she could show individuality through sport, language, and song. These were the great days of Irish leagues and societies: The Gaelic League, Cumann na nGaedheal, the Gaelic Athletic Association, the Phoenix Clubs, the Celtic Literary Society, and many others.[3]

[2]   Vivian Mercier. 'English Readers: Three Historical "Moments."' *Irish Writers and Politics*. Ed. Okimufi Komesu and Masaru Sekine. Savage, MD: Barnes and Noble, 1990. 18.

[3]   Brenna Katz Clarke. *The Emergence of the Irish Peasant Play at the Abbey Theatre*. Ann Arbor: UMI Press, 1982. 14.

At this time, a growing number of Irish reflected on their ancestral roots and sought the language that their English neighbors once denied them.[4] In fact, the Gaelic League's main objective, as articulated by Clarke, was 'to revive Irish as a spoken language as a means of proving to England that Ireland was a separate nation with a separate language.'[5] The goal of many Irish people was to develop a culture whose strength was its difference, and not its similarity, to that of England.

Evolving from the Irish National Theatre, which opened in Dublin in 1899, the Abbey's goals were different from its predecessor's. One of the most visible problems with the Irish National Theatre was that 'all the principal parts were played by English players,'[6] a fact the founders of the Abbey intended to rectify. The goals of this new theatre were outlined in a formal letter sent out by Lady Gregory, Yeats, and Martyn:

> We propose to have performed, in Dublin, in the spring of every year certain Celtic and Irish plays, which, whatever be their degree of excellence, will be written with a high ambition, and so build up a Celtic and Irish school of dramatic literature. We hope to find in Ireland an uncorrupted and imaginative audience, trained to listen by its passion for oratory, and believe that our desire to bring upon the stage the deeper thoughts and emotions of Ireland will ensure for us a tolerant welcome, and that freedom to experiment which is not found in the theatres of England, and without which no new movement in art or literature can succeed. We will show that Ireland is not the home of buffoonery and of easy sentiment, as it has been represented, but the home of an ancient idealism. We are confident of the support of all Irish people who are weary of misrepresentation, in carrying out a work that is outside all the political questions that divide us.[7]

The key words that surface in this letter are 'freedom' and 'misrepresentation'; for indeed, the purpose of the Abbey was, in a sense, to correct and alter the portraits of Irish characters on the dramatic stage and free the drama from formulaic anglicized styles.[8] It remains intriguing, then, that the Irish Renaissance as a whole influenced the leading public and political figures in reconceptualizing their nation. Ireland's

---

[4]   The issue of the displacement and erosion of the Gaelic language will be addressed at length in Chapter 3.

[5]   Clarke. 'The Emergence of the Irish Peasant Play'. 91.

[6]   Lennox Robinson. *Ireland's Abbey Theatre: A History 1899–1951*. London: Sidgwick and Jackson, 1951. 5

[7]   Ibid. 2.

[8]   The goals of the Directors were clearly different from those of their English benefactress, Miss Annie Horniman. While a number of critics have implicated her romantic feelings for Yeats—which were, incidentally, never reciprocated—Robinson notes that 'she loved art, loved the theatre, yet, if she didn't expect great value for her money, she wanted, at least, efficiency.' *Ireland's Abbey Theatre*. 88. In a letter dated 13 January 1906, Horniman explains to a friend, 'I know perfectly well that people think that the Abbey Theatre is a political "side-show"—if it were, I would have nothing to do with it.' Robinson, 48. This reinforces the idea that Horniman's designs for the Irish stage lay in the art of the dramatic movement and not in the subtext.

position as initially determined by English hegemony would now become challenged as a result of the counter-hegemonic movement perpetuated by the literati. Through the dramatic art form, the traditionally objectified Other (the Irish) sought to reposition themselves as Subject. This explains the active and at times aggressive approach of the early Abbey playwrights' attempt to vault the dominant discourse of England and establish a new, comprehensive dialectic of the oppressed. Despite the Abbey's shortcomings, this act of resistance must be applauded, for it laid the groundwork for an emergent Irish ideology stressing separateness and individuality from its imperial neighbor.

If accuracy of national type in the theatre was to be a primary objective for the Abbey players, and, if nationalism was to remain separate from artistic expression, or according to that, a component only of what defined the Irish consciousness, then we have to wonder what sparked the 'Playboy Riots' of 1907 and the 'Plough Riots' of 1926. When J.M. Synge's *The Playboy of the Western World* debuted at the Abbey on 26 January 1907, the audience erupted in unabashed dismay. In his journal entry written after the opening night's fracas, Abbey historiographer Joseph Holloway reports:

> The Abbey was thronged in the evening to witness the first performance of Synge's three-act comedy *The Playboy of the Western World*, which ended in fiasco owing to the coarseness of the dialogue. The audience bore with it for two and a half acts and even laughed with the dramatist at times, but an unusually brutally coarse remark[9] put into the mouth of 'Christopher Mahon,' the playboy of the title, set the house off into hooting and hissing amid counter applause, and the din was kept up till the curtain closed in.[10]

In retrospect, I believe that the disturbances were incited because of a misunderstanding; for Synge's depiction of accuracy strayed from what the Anglo-Irish, urban audience was accustomed to. Synge's character type was naturalistic to the population characterized in his play, while the blatantly disruptive reaction of the Dublin audience suggests a population whose romantic view of language asserts that accuracy was not one of their primary concerns. In particular, the Playboy Riots reflect a split between urban/country sensitivities that ironically reveal a nation fractured rather than unified by drama. Pertaining to this split, Said states of the Irish, 'The national bourgeoisie and their specialized elites ... in effect tended to replace the colonial force with a new class-based and ultimately exploitative one, which replicated the old colonial structures in new terms.'[11] While the Irish nation and people were originally stereotyped as 'uncivil' and 'barbarous,' these highbrow

---

[9]   The statement which caused the uproar was Christy's rebuttal to the Widow Quin: 'It's Pegeen I'm seeking only, and what'd I care if you brought me a drift of chosen females, standing in their shifts itself, maybe, from this place to the Eastern World.' 54. 'Shifts,' at this time in history, referred to nightgowns and was considered offensive by the Irish audience.

[10]   Joseph Holloway. *Abbey Theatre: A Selection From His Unpublished Journal, Impressions of a Dublin Playgoer.* Carbondale: Southern Illinois UP, 1967. 81.

[11]   Said. *Culture and Imperialism.* 223.

playgoers attributed the same stigmatism to the rural peasants. In essence, they are just as prejudiced as the English gentry.

Synge and the Abbey directorate were shocked by the audience's reaction to Synge's artistic vision of peasant life in the Aran Islands; but in turn-of-the-century Ireland, his style was incomprehensible to many theatergoers. With regard to the problematic scenes which sparked the reaction, 'The language is never obscene though the word "bloody" is used and a female garment is described as a "shift." The grotesque situation and those few words seem to be the only things to object to—if object you must—yet they caused a riot in the Theatre.'[12] Perhaps we only see the preposterousness of this attack on the playwright; for in the Age of Technology we have become numb to the violent images and explicit language that bombard our senses every day. But considering the date of the play (1907), the naturalistic dialogue of Western Ireland—which would be unfamiliar to Dubliners—the deep religious convictions of the Irish people, and the idea that the play's protagonist enjoys popularity with the townspeople for 'killing' his father, perhaps help us to understand the audience's inability to digest Synge's work. While disturbances continued throughout the play's tenure during its Abbey opening, the theatre was not without an audience each night as the Irish people were undoubtedly curious to see what provoked the violent reaction.

Synge ignited a controversy on the Abbey stage with his 'indecent' play, which has since become one of the most popular dramas of the past century in Ireland and abroad. Grappling with the unprovoked reaction from his Dublin audience, Synge wrote, 'It seems so impossible to get our Dublin people to see, obvious as it is—that the wildness and, if you will, vices of the Irish peasantry are due, like their extraordinary good points of all kinds, to the *richness* of their nature—a thing priceless beyond words.'[13] Here the playwright emphasizes that the diversity and variations of a culture must be examined to recognize its true value. Nevertheless, the fact that Synge's play presented a naturalistic representation of life in the secluded Aran Isles did not sit well with the city dwellers, and even the respected Irish biographer Sean O'Faolain approaches the peasant play[14] genre with furrowed brow:

> In the most creative 50 years of Anglo-Irish literature then (from about 1890–1940) the writers saw Irish life, in the main, romantically. It was as a poetic people that they first introduced themselves to the world, and it is as a poetic people that we are still mainly known abroad. The peasant plays of the Abbey Theatre, even when supposedly realistic, held still the charm of external novelty, dress, speech, situation, humour and were bathed in that sense of natural wonder which is best illustrated by the plays of Synge.[15]

---

[12]   Robinson. *Ireland's Abbey Theatre*. 52.
[13]   Clarke. *The Emergence of the Irish Peasant Play*. 165.
[14]   The peasant play constitutes a genre in Irish drama whereby characterizations of rural life strive to promote realistic portrayals of those Irish who face the harsh terrain of Ireland's landscape.
[15]   Quoted in Clarke, *The Emergence of the Irish Peasant Play*. 62.

Evidently, O'Faolain sees the emergence of the peasant play as a romantic portrayal of the rural Irish rather than the realistic portrait that Synge and others attempted to create. While O'Faolain believes that these plays were romanticized rather than realistic, with Synge in particular, tragedy often lies couched in the comic elements of the plays.

Within the nation of Ireland itself, there exist dominant discourses and as with practically any country, the dominant discourse is centered around cities such as Dublin. As a result, people who reside outside the locale of this preeminent group are considered to be less articulate. Stereotypes reek of lack of sophistication, and as we see through the example of the Irish, people who live in the peripheries (i.e. rural areas) are branded as lowbrows and thus denigrated to a lesser status. Hence Irish people living in the margins face a double jeopardy—they must overcome the hegemonic English discourse as well as the dominant discourse of their own land.

This issue falls into the debate over authentic representation at the Abbey, and in an article dated 26 November 1911,[16] Fred O'Donovan writes,

> The Irish Players wanted to put on the stage the real Irishman of today—to reveal real Irish conditions and real Irish character. Now, to reach the real Irish character, the poets and dramatists had to deal with the life of the peasantry, those who lived close to the soil and obtained their subsistence from it. The upper classes are veneered with English thought and manners, hence few of the plays which the Irish Players have presented deal with life in the cities—with business and social circles.[17]

From the inception of the Abbey, the actors attempted to expose and advance the discourse of the marginalized Irish. But for the Ascendancy,[18] this program undermined their support for the plays produced in Dublin. In other words, the very people whose lives were being portrayed were not represented in the audience.

When Sean O'Casey entered the Dublin dramatic circle in 1923,[19] issues of representation at the Abbey were once again raised. But this playwright, who once served as secretary of the Irish Citizen Army, added a new burst of energy in a stifled theater environment. Not since the days of Synge had the Abbey entertained the success and attention it found with O'Casey; he was just what the theater needed. O'Casey revitalized the Abbey Theatre with the theatrical debut of his *Three Plays*:

---

[16]   This article appeared in the New York publication *World* on page 6.

[17]   E.H. Mikhail. *The Abbey Theatre: Interviews and Recollections*. Totowa, NJ: Barnes and Noble. 10.

[18]   As defined by Cairns and Richards, the Ascendancy consisted of the Anglo-Irish 'who enjoyed access to political power in Ireland during the later seventeenth and eighteenth centuries. The Ascendancy comprised an amalgam of New English families, together with a few of the Old English ... who had conformed to Anglicanism and a very much larger number of descendants of colonists who had arrived during the Commonwealth (1649–60) or the subsequent Williamite/Jacobite struggles.' *Writing Ireland*. 167.

[19]   *Shadow of a Gunman*, O'Casey's first play at the Abbey, was produced on 9 April 1923.

Shadow of a Gunman, Juno and the Paycock, and *The Plough and the Stars.* While he wrote numerous others, he is best remembered for those three, and yet when *Shadow* opened on 12 April 1923, only the theatre critic from the *Evening Herald* saw the dramatist's potential:

> It was indeed a welcome and wholesome sign to sit in the Abbey last night and listen to an audience squirming with laughter and reveling boisterously in the satire which Mr. Sean O'Casey has put into his two-act play. Not for a very long time has such a good play come our way. It was brilliant truthful, decisive ... His characters were as perfect and his photography, for one really felt his men and women were but photographs, was nothing less than the work of genius.[20]

O'Casey's popularity with Dubliners steamrolled decisively, for when *Juno and the Paycock* opened on 3 March 1924, it broke all records and 'continued for a second week to satisfy the crowds turned away from the door.'[21] Instead of focusing on the peasant's life, O'Casey's plays depicted the meager existence of residents of the Dublin tenements, and while five of his plays[22] revolved around political strife in his native land, the dramatist had only a tenuous affiliation with the Irish Nationalist movement. 'Irish Nationalists were sensitive to the image of Ireland presented both abroad and at home. Like O'Casey later, Synge detested nationalistic abstractions and wanted to flatten the idealism of nationalism. For this reason, both he and O'Casey caused the greatest stir, despite the reality of their pictures—or perhaps because of them.'[23] Naturalism, and not a romanticized idealistic portrayal of Irish politics, got O'Casey into trouble.

As happened with his predecessor, rioting occurred in the first week of O'Casey's highly acclaimed play, *The Plough and the Stars.* The 'Plough Riots' are described first-hand by the author himself:

> The high, hysterical, distorted voices of women kept squealing that Irish girls were noted over the whole world for their modesty, and that Ireland's name was holy; that the Republican flag had never seen the inside of a public house; that this slander on the Irish race would mean the end of the Abbey Theatre; and that Ireland was Ireland through joy and through tears.[24]

Unlike the audience participation in the Playboy Riots which stemmed from disagreement over representation of Irish character, the fracas sparked by O'Casey's

---

[20]   Hugh Hunt. *The Abbey: Ireland's National Theatre 1904–1979.* New York: Columbia UP, 1979. 122.

[21]   Ibid. 123.

[22]   *Shadow of a Gunman* painted a picture of the Anglo-Irish War, while *Juno and the Paycock* alluded to The Civil War; *The Plough and the Stars* zeroed in on the Easter Rebellion of 1916, The Great War of 1914–1918 was the subject of *The Silver Tassie,* and *Red Roses for Me* portrayed the Lockout and Great Strike of 1913.

[23]   Clarke. *The Emergence of the Irish Peasant Play.* 164.

[24]   Hunt. *The Abbey.* 125.

play occurred because of audience disagreement over its historical/political events. While *The Playboy*'s indecency originated from the naturalistic language of the play, those who attacked *The Plough* included Mrs Sheehy-Skeffington, a leader in the Nationalist Movement, and Mrs Pearse, widow of Padraic, who was executed after the Easter Rising 1916.

These female nationalists created the uproar first because O'Casey put the national flag in the hands of the character of Rosie, a prostitute, in a pub, and second because Pearse and other statesmen involved in the uprising were not heroicized through this dramatic portrait of the events surrounding the insurrection. In fact, O'Casey purposely keeps the identity of the leader of the Citizen Army ambiguous and gives his character the title Voice of the Man. Therefore, the political hijacking of the play was incited largely through a misreading of its portrayal of historical events and its concept of 'honor.' Actress Shelah Richards adds, 'Some of us felt this was a betrayal: we were involved, the play was a masterpiece, O'Casey our hero and we were prepared to fight, literally, for him and his play. The pro-O'Caseyites summarily manned the curtain and brought it swinging down ... Meanwhile the Directors were being phoned all over Dublin.'[25] The great stir provoked a sense of nostalgia and patriotic sentiments, and regardless of how the audience reacted, their literalistic reception of The Plough and the Stars reflected the importance of drama for the Irish.

Gerard Fay explains the rationale behind the uproar associated with this great play: 'Since his theme was the freedom of Ireland, his very title taken from the banners of the Citizen Army, O'Casey was reluctant to have the police called ... The shouting sounded very much like what had been heard during "Playboy"—"an insult to Irish womanhood," "a slander against the good name of the Citizen Army".'[26] Following the commotion, it was Yeats's turn to address the audience: 'You have disgraced yourselves again. Is this to be an ever-recurring celebration of the arrival of Irish genius? Once more you have rocked the cradle of genius.'[27] In the end, Dublin theatergoers' failure to acknowledge 'the cradle of genius' in Ireland's up-and-coming dramatists hurt Yeats and wounded O'Casey as much as the audience disturbances.

Brush up your Shakespeare

One may wonder, then, why a literary movement so dedicated to distinguishing itself from its imperial neighbor would be so heavily influenced by the premier poet and playwright of that nation; for Shakespeare's voice resounds throughout much of the drama coming out of modern Ireland—not to mention his presence in Irish literature

---

[25]   Ibid. 126.

[26]   Gerard Fay. *The Abbey Theatre: Cradle of Genius*. Dublin: Clonmore and Reynolds, 1958. 147.

[27]   Ibid. 147; Yeats is referring to the Playboy Riots of 1907.

generally throughout the twentieth century. 'Shakespeare is not just some ideological tool by which a single dominant group reproduces its own cultural and economic hegemony';[28] moreover, as this study will demonstrate, he serves as a model for the oppressed groups in marginalized societies. For example, when Leopold Bloom, the protagonist in James Joyce's *Ulysses*, identifies Shakespeare as 'our national poet' (16.782), he intimates a paradoxical counter-hegemonic sympathy. Though normally considered England's 'national' poet and dramatist, Bloom's statement suggests that the Strafordian's works resonate with the Irish. Shakespeare writes passionately about the human condition—not merely the *English* human situation, but rather a transnational plight. Because of this quality in Shakespeare's plays, the English dramatist lends himself to appropriation *by* other nations.

For Yeats, Shakespeare's influence was pervasive. In fact, at the Abbey's opening on 27 December 1904, the first play to be staged (for Lady Gregory's *Spreading the News* was also performed that night) was Yeats's *On Baile's Strand*, a short piece that closely resembles Shakespeare's *King Lear* and contains allusions to the Weird Sisters in *Macbeth*. Both Shakespeare plays harbor nationalistic themes, as does Yeats's, which focuses on Cuchulain. As Declan Kiberd states:

> It is one thing to imitate your Shakespearian father; it is quite another to take the approach of Yeats and turn him into a revised version of yourself. Moreover, both Yeats and Synge were reaching back beyond the imperial mission to a pre-modern, carnivalesque vitality, to those elements which peoples shared before the fall into imperialism and nationalism— elements which survived in Shakespeare's plays, and which seemed to intersect, in suggestive ways, with the folk life of rural Ireland.[29]

Kiberd also provides insight into why Irish writers are engaged with Shakespeare's plays: 'Rereading England, the artists learned to rewrite Ireland, and so enabled an Irish Renaissance.'[30]

The rise and popularity of the Abbey Theatre in the early years of the 1900s and, consequently, its Irish dramatists coincide with a surge of nationalism in Ireland which was, in turn, heightened by an influx of political unrest, military upheaval, and patriotic martyrs. However, the Abbey was beleaguered by a pervading sense of failure; for the rioting that occurred first with Synge's *The Playboy of the Western World* and then with O'Casey's *The Plough and the Stars* revealed an obvious split between the binary dialectic of audience/artisan. This rift spoke of a fractured Ireland rather than an emergent nation. Yet the failure of the Abbey to suture the fragmented pieces represented by national/apolitical, urban/rural, Irish/Anglo-Irish dichotomies, and social class distinctions should not outweigh the merit of

---

[28]   Curtis Beight. 'Elizabethan World Pictures.' *Shakespeare and National Culture*. Ed. John J. Joughin. Manchester. Manchester UP, 1997. 297.

[29]   Declan Kiberd. *Inventing Ireland: The Literature of the Modern Nation*. Cambridge, MA: Harvard UP. 274.

[30]   Ibid. 281.

the theatre. This turbulent era sparked a new, keener perception of nationalism and identity-consciousness among the Irish and cannot be discussed without assessing the dramatic literature of this period and the formation of the Abbey. This project achieved in Dublin what the Globe Theatre created in Renaissance London—a stage where playwrights could voice their political and artistic convictions. However, the Abbey's failure was due to a kind of double jeopardy. The rift which increasingly exacerbated the dichotomies mentioned above stemmed from miscommunication; and in a nation whose very culture— i.e., language, traditions, and customs—has been stripped away by a hegemonic force, this repeated inability to establish a unified identity was understandable.

'A State of Chassis': Sean O'Casey's Dublin Plays and Shakespeare's *Henriad*

While a plethora of talented Irish writers such as William Butler Yeats, Lady Gregory and J.M. Synge achieved international recognition for themselves and their homeland in the modern drama movement, Sean O'Casey's poignant depictions of the struggle for cultural and social identity amidst political turmoil set him apart from his fellow dramatists. Certainly, a prevailing sense of nationalism and individuality is reflected in the literature of this period; but more so than any other genre, I would argue the drama of Ireland chronicles historically significant events that would influence the colonized nation's people and their political ideology in the years ahead.[31] In this context, the inscription of Shakespeare in these plays is occasioned by the shared interest in the construction of national identity. One Irish playwright in particular who incorporated this interest in both the Bard and national identity was Sean O'Casey, who taught himself to read after purchasing a complete edition of the *Works of Shakespeare*.[32] In *Juno and the Paycock* and *The Plough and the Stars*, which make up two-thirds of his Dublin Trilogy, O'Casey appropriates Shakespeare and specifically the *Henriad*. In doing so he reassesses the question posed by Captain Macmorris in *Henry V*: 'What ish my nation?'

Over the course of three previous centuries, Ireland's drama arguably failed to address the intricacies of forging a national identity. But with the overwhelming support of the Abbey Theatre in particular, Irish literary figures of the twentieth century were afforded the opportunity to stage exclusively Irish productions with

---

[31]   With the title character from *Juno and the Paycock* and Nora Clitheroe in *The Plough and the Stars*, Sean O'Casey offers a reconceptualization of those historical events focusing on the marginalized citizens of the tenements and not the accepted Irish nationalism of 1924/1926.

[32]   Lady Gregory, a close friend of O'Casey's until the Abbey Theatre rejected his play, *The Silver Tassie*, 'chronicled his early reading, noting that he memorized much of Shakespeare from a Globe Edition of the works which he bought for a shilling.' See Mary Fitzgerald's essay 'Sean O'Casey and Lady Gregory: The Record of a Friendship.' *Sean O'Casey: Centenary Essays*. Ed. David Krause and Robert G. Lowery. Gerrards Cross: Colin Smythe, 1980. 77.

sometimes controversial themes. Through the strident efforts of writers such as Yeats, Lady Gregory, Synge, and O'Casey, Dublin's dramatic production offered itself as an authoritative voice of Irish life that, unlike the novel, genuinely demonstrated the lives of Ireland's working class.[33] Drama of this period directly reflected Hamlet's proclamation, 'Suit the action to the word,/the word to the action ... to/hold as 'twere the mirror up to nature ... and the very age and body of the/time his form and pressure (III.ii.17–18, 21–24). Arguably, no Irish playwright showcased in the Abbey Theatre conveyed Shakespeare's instruction to 'hold the mirror up to nature' as triumphantly as Sean O'Casey; for his impoverished upbringing in the Dublin tenements provided him with the resources to inscribe naturalistic traits into his memorable characters.

With the single exception of Alice Fox Blitch,[34] many O'Casey scholars have, to a lesser extent, recognized the importance of Shakespeare to the Irish playwright, expounding on stylistic similarities, parallel goals and his professed adoration for the Stratfordian; I will consider the breadth of these cursory studies to assess Shakespeare's impact on O'Casey. First, Robert Hogan and Richard Burnham define O'Casey as neo-Elizabethan, proposing that:

> He lures us into the theatre under the pretext of affording us hearty laughter, which, sooth to say, he most profusely provokes, and he sends us away with tears in our eyes and with the impression of direst tragedy lying heavy on our hearts. None but a neo-Elizabethan could accomplish this, since the secret of juxtaposing and harmonising the comic with the tragic, and thereby throwing the elements of terror and pathos into greater relief, has been lost to the English speaking stage for over a couple of centuries. Moreover, one-half of the fascination of Mr. O'Casey's work lies in its red-hot throbbing contemporaneity, and that too was a prime trait of Elizabethan drama.[35]

For Hogan and Burnham, O'Casey's crafty blending of the tragic and the comic invokes the artistry of sixteenth-century England in a way that no playwright since Shakespeare has been able to accomplish with such success. Perhaps O'Casey can be dubbed a neo-Shakespearean just as easily, for no other Renaissance dramatist possessed the ability to transport the audience from one emotional extreme to another as Shakespeare did. Certainly, O'Casey inherits this creative ability. But what is initially hidden in their discussion and what is absolutely pertinent to this investigation are the analogies that can be made between Shakespeare and O'Casey with their reference to the fascination of O'Casey's work lying in 'red-hot throbbing

---

[33]   O'Casey's realism and authentic portrayals of the working class sparked the Plough Riots when *The Plough and the Stars* was first staged at the Abbey Theatre.

[34]   In her essay 'O'Casey's Shakespeare,' Blitch draws connections between *Juno and the Paycock* and *Henry IV*. Rather than investigate the larger nationalistic underpinnings that this chapter strives to uncover, Blitch's essay draws mainly on topical allusions between a variety of characters and focuses on comparative dramatic methodologies. *Modern Drama* 15 (1972): 283–90.

[35]   Robert Hogan and Richard Burnham. *The Years of O'Casey, 1921–1926: A Documentary History.* Gerrards Cross: Colin Smythe, 1992. 193.

contemporaneity.' Just like Shakespeare, Hogan and Burnham have discovered how much of O'Casey's work is tied to political underpinnings of his present-day Ireland.

In 'Sean O'Casey's Dublin Trilogy,' Ronald Ayling seeks to establish similarities in the critics' reception of both writers, stating that:

> Throughout the years a number of critics and scholars have fairly consistently attempted to prove that Shakespeare could not possibly have written the plays generally attributed to him; the primary grounds for their dissatisfaction appear to be those very qualities which, to some extent, he shared with the Irish writer: his humble origins and relative lack of formal education.[36]

This critical treatment of the writers' backgrounds seems a bit contrived; for it is the content of the plays, and not the playwright's origin, that is curious since Shakespeare's plays generally focus on the realpolitik of the aristocratic milieu. In contrast, O'Casey's plays could be said to echo his Dublin background as it exposes life in the urban slum dwellings. What is interesting about Ayling's account is his desire to prove Shakespeare's kinship with O'Casey; he seems to be suggesting— without discussing any textual appropriations—that O'Casey is his reincarnation.

In addition, the analogies are, according to Heinz Kosok, 'the clearest expression of [O'Casey's] admiration and his desire to be seen as a successor'[37] to Shakespeare. This may be true, as critics have also discussed the absolute adoration O'Casey had for Shakespeare, whom, according to his wife, 'was his god.'[38] In addition, the Irish playwright's affection for Shakespeare surfaces in numerous correspondences written over his lifetime. For example, O'Casey was so honored that two of his plays were chosen to be performed in England in 1964 on the occasion of Shakespeare's 400th jubilee that he expressed his sentiments in a letter to Peter Daubeny:

> The best way to honour him, of course … is to know and love him; but it is good and proper to honour him in a tribute from one who loves true men and true poets. You have done richly in assembling this tribute in London. I am grateful to you for thinking of a place for Ireland and for me among those who come bearing the gold, frankincense and myrrh of Drama as an offering to the Poet![39]

This letter yields the clearest evidence of the Irishman's adulation for Shakespeare, and here, O'Casey equates the Stratfordian with the Christ-child; thus, through his plays, Shakespeare becomes a Messianic figure/Muse for him. But more importantly and relevant to this study, O'Casey is accepted into a 'tribute in London' and therefore

[36]   Ronald Ayling. 'Sean O'Casey's Dublin Trilogy.' *Sean O'Casey: A Collection of Critical Essays.* Ed. Thomas Kilroy. Englewood Cliffs, NJ: Prentice-Hall, 1975. 14.
[37]   Heinz Kosok. *Sean O'Casey, The Dramatist.* Gerrards Cross: Colin Smythe, 1985. 346.
[38]   Ibid.
[39]   Quoted in ibid. 196.

conceives himself/Ireland as part of that national identity. This 'place for Ireland' and O'Casey at the celebration represents the British figuring of Shakespeare and the 'what ish my nation' question of Irish national identity.

O'Casey's fealty to Shakespeare stems from his early years; for it was through that first purchase of the Bard's plays that O'Casey learned how to read. Perhaps, surprisingly, he does better than 'learn' Shakespeare; he understands—and later appropriates—him. In fact, the Irish playwright boldly professes to have a better comprehension of the Elizabethan dramatist and his works than Shakespeare's own countrymen as evidenced in the first volume of *The Letters of Sean O'Casey 1910–1941*. In a letter dated 31 May 1939 to Mikhail Alpetin, secretary of the Foreign Commission of Writers' Union of the USSR, O'Casey castigates the English for their inability to grasp the true nature of Shakespeare. He recounts:

> The English had a Shakespeare Festival of a week or so in the Memorial Theatre in Stratford on Avon (where the poet was born); a place where only those who have a lot of money and time on and in their hands can go. One theatre in London—called the Old Vic gives performances of Shakespeare's plays constantly. Some of these are done well, and many of them are done badly — The bare truth is that Shakespeare is nor wept nor sung nor honoured in his own country. As for the workers, it may be said that they never come into touch with Shakespeare from the cradle to the grave. Millions and millions have never seen a play of his, and he has been so neglected that very few actors are able to play a principle character in any of his plays ... By the way, dear friend, I'm an Irishman, and it's rather amusing that an Irishman should have to rebuke England for the stupid neglect of one of her greatest sons.[40]

O'Casey's dissatisfaction with the representation of Shakespeare on the English stage is twofold: first, while indicting Shakespeare's countrymen for their inadequate portrayals of these plays, O'Casey clearly feels that they are not accessible—as they should be—to the working-class. Conversely, this letter implies that the misrepresentation of Shakespeare occurs because of the undiscerning highbrow audience with its devotion to leisurely pursuits. Secondly, it criticizes those representations for their failure to incorporate Shakespeare as an integral part of national identity. As this study illustrates, O'Casey makes Shakespeare available not only to all socio-economic groups, but to a variety of nationalities as well.

Although scholarship on O'Casey has acknowledged Shakespearean references in his work, studies have failed to appreciate the depth of these allusions. If we were to look retrospectively at Ireland's historiography, we would find it intertwined with a strong political ideology—especially in the early twentieth century. And within this matrix, O'Casey, like his Elizabethan predecessor, uses his stagecraft to chronicle Ireland's more recent history. In fact, the majority of O'Casey's Dublin Trilogy (I'm excluding *The Shadow of a Gunman* from this study) figures like Shakespeare's most popular history play cycle—*1 Henry IV*, *2 Henry IV*, and *Henry V*—and this

---

40   David Krause, ed. *The Letters of Sean O'Casey, 1910–41*. New York: Macmillan, 1975. 801–2.

study analyzes this phenomenon in detail. Ronald Ayling addresses this very issue comprehensively:

> [O'Casey's] plays, though self-contained and complete in themselves, are more meaningful in conjunction with the other plays relating to their particular cycle, and, together with them, add up to a panoramic view of a country in a state of crisis. Of course Shakespeare's plays are more consciously shaped as chronicles of an age, a particular period of history, than are O'Casey's. Starting to write at a time when there was an immense popular demand for history plays, Shakespeare took an evolving genre that only a few years earlier had been little more than crude two-dimensional representation of historical and legendary figures and widened the social context to embrace many different levels of society and regional ways of life. At the same time, while he humanised and individualised his narrative sources, Shakespeare depicted history with an awareness that a moral design was to be discerned in it. Beginning from the opposite end, as it were, O'Casey wrote of the lives and struggles of ordinary men and women at a particular time of social upheaval, and in the process gave the drama something of an epic compass, realising a social and political content that is far wider and deeper than is apparent at first sight.[41]

While Shakespeare represents the marginalized nationalities in his *Henriad* and yolks together the Irish, Welsh, and Scots as strategically focused under the leadership of the 'English' Henry V, he focuses on these peripheral identities/regions for different reasons than O'Casey does in 1926; for we are talking about two different historical epochs. Yet while Ayling's perceptions are cogent, he overextends the Bard's universally transcendental qualities and fails to consider the relevance of the history plays to world events in the present. Consider, for example, Winston Churchill's personal solicitation of Laurence Olivier to create a film based on *Henry V* to promote patriotism during World War II, and the highly successful adaptation of *Henry V* by Kenneth Branagh which was prompted by events in the Falklands.

O'Casey and Shakespeare challenge two inherent cultural dichotomies in their respective societies: religion/politics and chaos/order. O'Casey, like Shakespeare, illustrates how the tensions between the political and religious arenas contribute to the overall chaos in his nation, but ultimately suggests a sense of order imposed through a unification of national identities.

Dublin serves as a dreary landscape throughout twentieth-century Irish literature in the works of poets William Butler Yeats and Patrick Kavanaugh, novelists and short-story writers Flann O'Brien and James Joyce, and especially in the dramatic works of Sean O'Casey. This capital city's rich history coupled with its high poverty level[42] invites artists to reveal the state of chaos that engulfs their beloved Ireland

---

[41]   Ayling. 'Sean O'Casey's Dublin Trilogy.' 77–8.

[42]   Deirdre Henchy explains that by 1914, '34 percent of the population of Dublin was living below the poverty level' and even more startling statistics show that 'a third of the city was living in only 5000 tenement houses, 78 percent of which were one-roomed dwellings.' 'Dublin in the Age of O'Casey: 1880–1910.' *Essays on Sean O'Casey's Autobiographies*. Ed. Robert G. Lowery. Totowa, NJ: Barnes and Noble, 1981.

to the outside world. Dublin is 'a world poised constantly on the brink of disaster and yet sustained by a comic impulse, the ability to take serious matters and see the humor in them,' thus undermining potentially devastating situations and distancing the characters from their impact[43]. While this definition certainly holds true for O'Casey's highly publicized Dublin plays, we can identify Shakespeare as the progenitor for this motif in drama starting with *1 Henry IV*. As we see with the first play in the Henry cycle, Falstaff—representing the 'lord of misrule'—continuously rebuffs Hal's regal father through mockery and jests; in fact, he even assumes the role of surrogate to the hedonistic prince. While the issues Hal faces are serious, such as the threat of insurrection, the people he surrounds himself with provide comic relief from the tenuous life at court.

O'Casey's characters in *Juno and the Paycock* and *The Plough and the Stars* share at least one common denominator—they each reside in sparse quarters in Dublin's ill-cared-for slums. In addition, the dramatist's texts expose the political struggles that the Irish, both Protestant and Catholic, encounter daily. These inhibiting obstacles—British imperialism, religious tensions and poverty—lead the sympathetic characters to a dead end, for O'Casey portrays the working class in Dublin as the victim of political turmoil.[44] In this context, it is evident that the urban space serves as a detrimental component in the chaotic state of Ireland's capital city. O'Casey's graphic sketch of his hometown serves as a reflection of the state of the nation as a whole; for in his plays, the dramatist uncovers the harsh lifestyle of living in Dublin both before and after the Easter Rising of 1916.

The debut of O'Casey's *Juno and the Paycock* at the Abbey Theatre in 1924 met with an enthusiastic reception by its Dublin audience. The play focuses on the Boyle family, which consists of the lazy lover of drink 'Captain' Jack; his wife Juno, who provides some semblance of normalcy in her family unit; their daughter Mary, a lover of books who is symbolically associated with the Blessed Virgin; and Johnny, their disabled son whose military involvement leads to a doomed end. While the Boyles may appear to be dysfunctional, they provide a stark representation of the difficulties incurred by the Irish working class.

Heinz Kosok has declared that while 'Shakespeare is occasionally referred to as a model for O'Casey's plays ... there is only one brief study that supports such an assertion with proper evidence.'[45] However I would contend that the influence of the great English dramatist and poet on Sean O'Casey cannot be contested or

---

[43]   Mashey Bernstein. '"What a Parrot Talks": The Janus Nature of Anglo-Irish Writing.' *The Text and Beyond: Essays in Literary Linguistics.* Ed. Cynthia Golden Bernstein. Tuscaloosa: University of Alabama Press, 1994. 275.

[44]   Colbert Kearney. 'Sean O'Casey and the Glamour of Grammar.' *Anglo-Irish and Irish Literature: Aspects of Language and Culture.* Proceedings of the Ninth International Congress of the International Association for the Study of Anglo-Irish Literature Held at Uppsala University, 4–7 August 1986. Vol. 2. Ed. Birgit Bramsback and Martin Croghan. Stockholm: Almqvist and Wiksell International, 1988. 63.

[45]   Kosok. *Sean O'Casey.* 345.

minimized. In fact, the critic seemingly contradicts himself, for he mentions Shakespearean allusions in O'Casey's plays on several occasions. A point of further argument exists in Kosok's statement that 'Falstaff has been seen as a model for O'Casey's comic heroes, especially Captain Boyle, the closest approximation to Falstaff in contemporary literature.'[46] While Falstaff's presence in O'Casey's *Juno and the Paycock* is indeed overt, I argue that the famous sack-lover is resurrected in Joxer Daly, not Boyle. In fact, O'Casey's tragi-comedy, serving as an appropriation of Shakespeare's *1 Henry IV*, is equipped not only with the juxtaposition of Joxer/ Falstaff, but associates Captain Boyle with Prince Hal and Juno with King Henry IV. These relationships feed off the two dichotomies which encompass both texts (religion/politics and chaos/order) which will be the focus of a preliminary analysis.

Kosok states that O'Casey hailed Falstaff as the greatest character ever to appear on stage, and also suggested that 'this pre-eminent model has certainly helped to transform his acquaintances from the Dublin slums into the almost lovable good-for-nothings and braggarts of his plays.'[47] This transformation is manifested through the characterization of Joxer Daly, Boyle's instigating sidekick, who draws for the audience sundry parallels with Shakespeare's fat knight. Notice the entrance of O'Casey's 'shoudher-shruggin' Joxer' (10): 'Joxer steps cautiously into the room. He may be younger then the Captain but he looks a lot older. His face is like a bundle of crinkled paper; his eyes have a cunning twinkle ... His face is invariably ornamented with a grin' (11). Boyle's drinking 'butty' invokes images of Shakespeare's Falstaff from the beginning of the play, for Prince Hal's critical and lengthy description of him in his introductory scene in *1 Henry IV* breeds some noticeable similarities:

> Thou art so fat-witted with drinking of old
> sack, and unbuttoning thee after supper, and sleeping
> upon benches after noon, that thou hadst forgotten to
> demand that truly which thou wouldst truly know.
> What a devil hast thou to do with the time of the day?
> unless hours were cups of sack, and minutes capons,
> and clocks the tongues of bawds, and dials the signs of
> leaping-houses, and the blessed sun himself a fair hot
> wench in flame-color'd tafetta; I see no reason why thou
> shouldst be so superfluous to demand the time
> of the day. (I.ii.2–12)

The observations of both Joxer and Falstaff yield a definite parallel, for although O'Casey's stage directions provide minimal clues as to Joxer's appearance—compared to the copious lines throughout the *Henriad* that indicate the physicality of Falstaff—we can establish the general countenance of both characters to be old-looking, and pleasant. These fops exude contentment with life because of perpetual

---

[46]   Ibid.
[47]   Ibid.

intoxication, and both keep a merry disposition throughout their respective plays. Like Falstaff, Joxer's identification with time is just as careless, and he plays a key role in delaying Boyle's going to work. As Blitch asserts, 'Falstaff, as is universally recognized, extenuates Hal's unconventional behavior. Similarly, Joxer helps us to tolerate Boyle's neglect of his family.'[48] In sum, both show an utter disregard for responsibility—and this mentality seems infectious to their counterparts.

The analogies the audience may recognize in Joxer's and Falstaff's appearances delve much deeper than the physical, for Joxer's philosophies on life run closely in sync with Jack's. Perhaps one of Falstaff's most crucial passages in Shakespeare's *1 Henry IV* appears in V.iv.115–21: 'To die is to be a counterfeit, for he is but the counterfeit of a man who hath not the life of a man; but to counterfeit dying, when a man thereby liveth, is to be no counterfeit, but the true and perfect image of life indeed. The better part of valor is discretion, in the which better part I have sav'd my life.' This self-profession immediately follows Falstaff's cowardly deed; he pretends to be killed in battle to avoid a struggle with the Earl of Douglas and thus limits the possibility of being mortally wounded. O'Casey draws on Falstaff's cowardice in the form of Joxer when he responds incredulously in true Falstaffian fashion to Boyle's request to look out the window and survey the commotion outside: 'An' mebbe get a bullet in the kisser? Ah, none o' them thricks for Joxer! It's betther to be a coward than a corpse!' (20). Falstaff's discourse at the battle of Shrewsbury echoes throughout O'Casey's tragi-comedy as both O'Casey's *Juno* and Shakespeare's *1 Henry IV* depict Joxer and Falstaff as individuals who are concerned with self-preservation and frivolity rather than with the political upheavals that envelope their respective territories. In particular, Shakespeare and O'Casey illustrate this apoliticism as a means of commenting on the dichotomy between the serious attitudes towards conflict and the comic elements contained in characters who subvert such highbrow posturing.

Another noticeable link between these two comic figures resides in the way both are treated by their 'friends'; when Boyle fancies a pint in the snug, he desires Joxer's companionship, just as Hal frolics with Falstaff to escape the constraints of court. Interestingly, Joxer is abandoned for a time by Boyle just as Hal casts away Falstaff—although the latter becomes a permanent separation. Boyle says he's 'done with Joxer' (29) after the articulate, handsome Charlie Bentham reveals that he has inherited a large sum of money from a cousin. Boyle comes to the realization that he is a new man and, like a true 'paycock,' feels superior to his cohort. Stepping into this new persona, Boyle informs Joxer 'it's a responsibility, Joxer, a great responsibility' to have money (31). Oddly enough, both Boyle and Hal sense that when responsibilities arise, they recognize the burden this new power brings—in their cases, they abandon friends who have contributed to their drunken revelry. Of course, Prince Hal's responsibility is much greater and much more serious than Boyle's, but his harsh repudiation of Falstaff leaves an unpalatable taste in

---

48   Blitch. 'O'Casey's Shakespeare.' 284.

the audience's mouth. When Hal gains his father's good graces once again, 'plump Jack' is of no value to him, and all he can say is 'I know thee not, old man' (*2 Henry IV*, V.v.47). Furthermore, both Joxer and Falstaff are ready to take credit for what others do; O'Casey's anti-hero is willing to drop off those three pounds in Act II for Boyle's well-being[49] just as Falstaff takes credit for Hotspur's death.[50] Both characters consort with Boyle/Hal looking for a reward. In addition, Joxer's lines about standing up to Juno 'facin' fearful odds' (24) resonates with Falstaff's lies about fighting off two or three and fifty' in Act II.iv.187 and again in the episode with Hotspur's corpse. Neither lives up to the bravery they preach; rather, Joxer jumps out the window when Juno comes home and Falstaff plays dead on the battlefield.

The connections between O'Casey's *Juno* and Shakespeare's *1 Henry IV* do not end with the characters of Falstaff and Joxer; for like Jack, Joxer plays sidekick to an individual with a sense of authority who attempts to escape from his duties. Boyle acts very much like Shakespeare's troubled Prince Hal, for he takes his office lightly and cavorts daily with his friends, drinking and shirking his responsibilities. Consider Juno's chastisement of her husband: 'Ah, then, me boyo, you'd do far more work with a knife an' fork than ever you'll do with a shovel! If there was e'er a genuine job goin' you'd be dh' other way about—not able to lift your arms with the pains in your legs!' (13). Juno's words may prompt laughter from the audience, but the condition in the Boyle household is serious, and until the Captain realizes this, their lives will be in a 'terrible state o' chassis' (73). Interestingly, while Captain Boyle can by no means be considered royalty, he holds a title that commands respect, even though he does not deserve it, and the same can be said for Hal. King Henry laments Hal's choices in life, and proclaims 'I … /See riot and dishonor stain the brow/Of my young Harry' (I.i.84–6). Boyle's and Hal's titles remain hollow until (or if) they embrace responsibility.

Like the parallels exemplified between Joxer and Falstaff, the similarities between Boyle and Hal go deeper into the nature of these individuals and the situations they find themselves in. For example, consider the King's afflicted words to his son in *1 Henry IV*:

---

49   Joxer nonchalantly suggests, 'I've just dhropped in with the [3 pounds, 5 shillings] that Mrs. Madigan riz on the blankets an' table for you, an' she says you're to be in no hurry payin' it back.' 32.

50   Falstaff claims, 'There is/Percy [throwing the body down]. If your father will do/me any honor, so; if not, let him kill the next Percy/himself' (V.iv.139–42).

Tell me else,
Could such inordinate and low desires,
Such poor, such bare, such lewd, such mean attempts,
Such barren pleasures, rude society,
As thou art match'd withal grafted to,
Accompany the greatness of thy blood,
And hold their level with thy princely heart? (III.ii.11–18)

Just as King Henry IV exhibits frustration with his son, Hal, Juno is 'always grousin'(11) her husband Boyle for his foppish behavior and his choice of companions. Herein lies another connection between the two plays—for Juno, as ruler (or queen) of her household in the Dublin tenements, bears affinity to King Henry IV, leader of England. Both characters attempt to keep their charges, Boyle and Hal, under control and try to break them away from their foolish friends—Joxer and Falstaff. When gainful employment looms on Boyle's horizon, he is nowhere to be found, and Juno regretfully states, 'he's wherever Joxer Daly is—dhrinkin' in some snug or another' (9). Similarly, in *1 Henry IV* the King finds his son in a comparable predicament; while the court prepares for civil strife, the wrathful monarch indicts Hal for ambling 'up and down/With shallow jesters, and rash bavin wits ... Mingled his royalty with cap'ring fools' (III.ii.60–63). Both Juno and King Henry IV serve as agents of order in their attempts to make Boyle and Hal dependable in a state of crisis.

In O'Casey's play, Act I ends with a reenactment of sorts of Prince Hal's confrontation with his father, who listens to the outpouring of the King's heart and responds, 'I shall hereafter, my thrice gracious lord,/Be more myself' (III.ii.92–3); likewise, after Juno admonishes Joxer, Boyle proclaims, 'He'll never blow the froth off a pint o' mine age, that's a sure thing ... I'm a new man from this out' (30). Analogous to Hal's relationship with his father in Shakespeare's history play, Juno and Boyle come together for a time in celebration of their inheritance. But Juno's tragic conclusion appears far removed from the gallant victory at Shrewsbury that serves as the finale of *1 Henry IV*, and perhaps O'Casey ends the play with a 'state o' chassis' (73) as a means of illustrating the predicament of Dublin, and more largely, the turbulence that pervades Ireland as a result of imperial deculturation.[51] Therefore, O'Casey's play attempts to forge an emergent discourse by commandeering Shakespeare's characters appropriated to Ireland's own ideological ends.

Strange Bedfellows: Religion and Politics

Promulgating an emergent national identity is no easy undertaking; for in *Culture and Imperialism*, Edward Said contends,

---

[51]   The chaotic discord in Dublin which serves as the backdrop of this play is caused largely by the Civil War that precipitated the partitioning of Northern Ireland and the Republic. What compounded this state of disarray even further was the unwelcome presence of the Black and Tans, the English soldiers.

to read most cultural deconstructionists, or Marxists, or new historicists is to read writers whose political horizon, whose historical location is within a society and culture deeply enmeshed in imperial domination. Yet little notice is taken of this horizon, few acknowledgements of the setting are advanced, little realisation of the imperial closure itself is allowed for.[52]

For Shakespeare, his society was the artificer and perpetuator of the colonization of the Other, whereas O'Casey's Ireland was the Object of the imperialist's push for new territorial conquests. As previously mentioned, the resulting turmoil amidst the political horizon is explicated in both Shakespeare's and O'Casey's texts through the dichotomies between religion and politics and chaos and order. At the same time, the dramatists offer a subtextual critique of a religion that is subservient to politics. Relative to Elizabethan England's position on this issue, Annabel Patterson posits 'the interinvolvement of political and religious repression in the second phase of Elizabeth's reign' elucidates 'a confusion that the government was concerned not to make visible to the public.'[53] One must question, however, how, following Henry VIII's shift from Catholicism to Anglicanism and subsequent excommunication from the papacy, the society under his daughter's reign could fail to recognize this didactic 'interinvolvement.' That being said, the inability to talk about religion outside of political debate has haunted Ireland for centuries—especially in the Northern counties—and therefore there is no way to avoid the day-to-day controversy.

O'Casey's castigation of the Catholic Church and, perhaps, organized religion in general, originates from his Protestant upbringing among the Catholic majority in Dublin's low-income dwellings. Within the Boyle family, a distinction appears between the ultra-religious Johnny, who fanatically insists on keeping the votive lit underneath the Virgin Mary at all times, and Mary, who appears to choose politics over religion from the onset of the play. For example, the stage directions inform that this twenty-two year old is 'well-made and good-looking,' and that '[t]wo forces are working in her mind—one, through the circumstances of her life, pulling her back; the other, through the influence of books she has read, pushing her forward' (5). But perhaps the most revealing window into the heart of Mary is described in the following discourse:

> *Mary (tying a ribbon fillet-wise around her head)*: I don't like this ribbon, ma; I think I'll wear the green—it looks betther than the blue.
> *Mrs Boyle*: Ah, wear whatever ribbon you like, girl, only don't be botherin' me. I don't know what a girl on strike wants to be wearin' a ribbon round her head for, or silk stockin's on her legs either; it's wearin' them things that make the employers think

---

52   Said, *Culture and Imperialism*. 66.
53   Patterson, *Reading Holinshed's* Chronicles. 129.

they're givin' yous too much money.

Mary: The hour is past now when we'll ask the employers' permission to wear what we like. (7)

On the brink of defining herself as a radical, Mary appears confident and aware of her emergence as an actively questioning, political woman who represents the new Ireland; she is not afraid to speak her mind. But the most telling action in this scene is her choice of the green ribbon over the blue. Symbolically, the color blue has long been associated with the Virgin Mary;[54] therefore, Mary's choice of the green one, a color representing Ireland, reveals her fading religious convictions in favor of secular ones. But Boyle's and Joxer's critique of the clergy is much less subtle:

Boyle: If they do anything for you, they'd want you to be livin' in the Chapel ... I'm goin' to tell you somethin', Joxer, that I wouldn't tell to anybody else—the clergy always had too much power over the people in this unfortunate country.

Joxer: It's dangerous, right enough.

Boyle (becoming enthusiastic): Didn't they prevent the people in '47 from seizin' the corn, an' they starvin'; didn't they down Parnell; didn't they say that hell wasn't hot enough nor eternity long enough to punish the Fenians? We don't forget, we don't forget them things, Joxer. If they've taken everything else from us, Joxer, they've left us our memory. (22)

Once Boyle hears of his inheritance, he will 'forget all these injustices ... yet the author himself is in deadly earnest in this indictment of the political and economic betrayal of the Irish people by their clergy.'[55] Similarly, this ideology surfaces in *2 Henry IV*; Morton confides in Northumberland,

> But now the Bishop
> Turns insurrection to religion.
> Suppos'd sincere and holy in his thoughts,
> He's follow'd both with body and mind;
> And doth enlarge his rising with the blood
> Of fair King Richard, scrap'd from Pomfret stones;
> Derives from heaven his quarrel and his cause;
> Tells them he doth bestride a bleeding land,
> Gasping for life under great Bullingbrook,
> And more and less do flock to follow him. (I.i.200–9)

---

54   The symbolism associated with the color blue appears in *The Dictionary of Christian Lore and Legend*. Ed. J.C.J. Metford. London: Thames and Hudson, 1983. The definition states: 'A colour associated with St. Mary the virgin, who is often depicted wearing a blue dress or mantle although the liturgical colour fixed her feasts in the 16th century was white. Blue may have become popular because of its heavenly or sentimental associations.' 52.

55   Ayling. 'Sean O'Casey's Dublin Trilogy.' 79–80.

Like the clergy attacked in *Juno*, Shakespeare's characters sense the problematic influence of the religious hierarchy on the political spectrum.

Chaos and disorder pervade *Juno and the Paycock* in a number of ways, and thus, appear to take cue from Shakespeare's *1 and 2 Henry IV*. Boyle's exclamation in the first act reveals his nonchalant attitude about the predicament he finds himself in: 'Ah, I suppose it's just the same everywhere—the whole worl's in a state o' chassis!' (18). But chaos begins in his own home, as the Boyle apartment—through its disarray—directly reflects the state of the world beyond the walls of the tenement building. For example, when Charlie Bentham arrives at the Boyle's abode to share news of the Will, Juno exclaims, 'You must excuse th' state o' th' place, Mr. Bentham; th' minute I turn me back that man o' mine always makes a litther o' th' place, a litther o' th' place' (26). Thus, the untidy home serves first, as a rendering of the Boyles' disordered lives and second, as a replica of the Dublin environment.

Shakespeare's plays elicit this same effect, and perhaps the most poignant rendering of chaos in *1 Henry IV* comes through Falstaff's words to fellow vagrant Bardolph:

Why, there is it. Come sing me a bawdy song,
make me merry. I was as virtuously given as a
gentleman need to be, virtuous enough: swore
little, dic'd not above seven times—a week, went to a
bawdy-house not above once in a quarter—of an hour,
paid money that I borrow'd—three or four times,
liv'd well and in good compass, and now I live out of
all order, out of all compass. (III.iii.13–19)

The disorder of Boyle's domestic space can be equated with that of Falstaff's physical space; for here the disordered body mirrors the chaotic body politic which is also 'out of all order.' Falstaff's person, then, serves as a metaphor for the chaotic political body. The nation is run by a monarch, Henry IV, who underhandedly deposed the original 'divine' king, Richard II, and the prince would rather consort among the seedier characters of London than live up to his responsibility as heir apparent.

With the chaos and disjointedness inherent in the cultural environment of these plays as well as the dramatists' own societies, a certain order does evolve. More specifically, a unification arises out of the disordered lives of the characters. For example, in the final act of *Juno and the Paycock* the action indicates that things cannot possibly get worse: the truth of the botched Will is disclosed, Mary discovers she's pregnant, Bentham has deserted her, and it is obvious that Johnny will have to pay for his sins with his life. However, Juno—through her female potency—imposes her own order on the situation:

Mrs Boyle: We'll go. Come, Mary, an' we'll never come back here agen. Let your father furrage for himself now; I've done all I could an' it was all no use—he'll be hopeless till the end of his days. I've got a little room in me sisther's where we'll stop till your

throuble is over, an' then we'll work together for the sake of the baby.
Mary: My poor little child that'll have no father!
Mrs Boyle: It'll have what's far betther—it'll have two mothers. (71)

O'Casey exposes a harsh truth in this particular scene; for Mary's child will grow up in an environment with more stability with two women caretakers. Surprisingly perhaps, the female characters in O'Casey's Dublin Trilogy and Shakespeare's *Henriad* are the imposing agents of order for the other characters. In Shakespeare's plays, for example, both Lady Hotspur and Mortimer's Welsh wife offer solace and a sense of clarity to the men who prepare to raise arms against the monarch in *1 Henry IV*; while Mistress Quickly regulates the customers' dallyings at the Boar's Head Tavern in *2 Henry IV*. In addition, the French princess Katherine becomes the instigator/focus of order between two imperial forces in *Henry V*. As illustrated with O'Casey's unforgettable characterization of female independence, Juno is the only hope for harmonizing the lives of her family members; and in *The Plough and the Stars*, Bessie Burgess, though not initially liked by her neighbors, alleviates the chaos for all who reside in her tenement.

Women in Irish literature, and especially throughout the twentieth century, have been characterized as strong, independent, and the controlling faction of their households. 'What has received comparatively little attention … is the role of Irish women in that struggle [for Irish nationality and identity] and how they themselves defined and sought to shape "the conscience of [the] race".'[56] Certainly, Irish women served as loyal nationalists, proponents of the suffragist movement, and political activists who rallied alongside their male counterparts in their quest for a unified national identity.

Just as importantly, O'Casey's reappropriation of the *Henriad* and women's place in it has important political resonances. For the scene between Mary and Mrs Boyle implies that all cannot be returned to order while Ireland is still divided and is still coping with English ideological imperialism imposed on Irish emergent national identity. Moreover, the child who is abandoned by the father serves as a metaphor for Irish national identity. Mary's child seems to be the essential symbol for Ireland's state as a new nation emerging from English hegemony—and hence without a father. Shakespeare suggests that whereas Hal rises to the status of national fatherhood, O'Casey's reconceptualization reveals an Ireland that still requires a complete national identity—not a Bentham who runs off to England. Mary, the informed emblem of Ireland's past and hope for the future, has a child with no father—symbolic of a unified nationalism that does not hide from itself within the dominant ideologies of England. Ireland's heroes have defeated English rule, but must now define themselves.

More specifically, the scenario which leaves Mary pregnant and abandoned by the baby's father ties into C.L. Innes's proclamation that 'there was a need for

---

[56]   C.L. Innes. *Woman and Nation in Irish Literature and Society, 1880–1935*. Athens, GA: The University of Georgia Press, 1993. 3.

a commitment to an Irish identity, the declaration of a relationship by birth and inheritance and passed from the motherland to her would-be children who needed to prove themselves her rightful heirs' (27). O'Casey inscribes his emergent national identity in his female characters who will fashion order through a chaos perpetuated by the male characters. While 'Ireland is frequently allegorized as a woman' to depict 'political and economic relationships with a male England,'[57] 'Irish nationalists and unionists even more frequently depict Ireland as a lady in distress.'[58] But Sean O'Casey subverts these pervasive images and stereotypes through his portrayal of the independent Juno.

Sean O'Casey's tragicomic *Juno and the Paycock* yields too many references to Shakespeare's *1 Henry IV* to be glossed over or easily dismissed by critics such as Kosok. It is paramount that we consider why O'Casey would rework perhaps the most famous of the Bard's English history plays into an Irish context. The Dublin dramatist's professed adoration for Shakespeare has much to do with the acknowledgement that the political upheavals that have become such a part of Ireland share a common bond with those found in Shakespeare's history plays. During the time Shakespeare was writing in Elizabethan England, this imperial force had to be cautious of other Western forces, and especially France and Spain. Although England defeated the Spanish Armada nearly a decade before the *Henriad* was complete—a feat that gained her international recognition as a dominant nation—the threat of conquest remained. This 'threat' of conquest is a perpetual reality for O'Casey's Ireland and we can identify the political parallels between the two countries, despite their separate historical epochs, in terms of invasion/assimilation. Furthermore, Elizabeth had no heir apparent and as her reign progressed, questions spread across the kingdom as to who would ascend the most powerful throne in the world. The fact that James VI, a Scotsman, was a possibility also raised questions regarding national identity. As discussed previously, Ireland's identity consciousness and preoccupation with the ruling order emerges through its literature, and becomes especially pronounced in its drama.

In his historical account of the Abbey Theatre, Gerard Fay offers, 'It is the pattern of drama in English-speaking countries to produce their best new plays and writers in times of national emotional excitement and stress.'[59] This notion is certainly reflected in the literature of Renaissance and Irish dramatists. O'Casey, in particular, produced his most popular works in a nationally volatile time; Ireland's civil war and the signing of the Treaty which ultimately allowed for the division between Northern Ireland and the Republic of Ireland coincides with the dating of O'Casey's Dublin trilogy. The Bard figures as a cultural agent who 'is imagined negotiating relations between literature and politics which largely unproblematically equate with present

---

57   Ibid. 10.
58   Ibid. 15.
59   Fay. *Cradle of Genius*. 151.

cultural environments.'[60] O'Casey's affinity for Shakespeare in this regard is best expressed in *The Plough and the Stars*, which endures as the richest component of the trilogy in terms of exacting the complexities of Ireland's national agenda.

First produced in 1926 at the Abbey Theater, *The Plough and the Stars* depicts events surrounding the Easter Uprising of 1916 in an often humorous, but ultimately tragic, manner. While the play's thematic inferences include forging Socialist views and a critique of the exploitation of the poor working-class, O'Casey's *Plough* also serves as an appropriation of Shakespeare's *Henry V* in an attempt to answer the question 'What ish my nation?' posited by the Elizabethan playwright's Captain Macmorris four centuries earlier. Opening with the banter of unlikely cronies—the foppish Fluther Good, the curmudgeon Peter, and propagandist The Covey—Act I foregrounds the social tensions existing in Dublin at the time of the insurrection and poses questions of identity amongst the characters. As a discussion ensues with regard to a political demonstration to muster support for the Irish Citizen Army,[61] Fluther innocently ponders, 'We're all Irishmen, anyhow; aren't we?' (143) as The Covey criticizes the meeting's purpose. But the young Covey retorts, 'Look here, comrade, there's no such thing as an Irishman, or an Englishman, or a German or a Turk; we're all only human bein's. Scientifically speakin', it's all a question of the accidental gatherin' together of mollycewels an' atoms' (143). This may speak to a similar 'state of chaos' of nationalism in which individual nations are unified by chance.

Thus, this scene indicates the same tension exemplified through Fluther, The Covey and Peter that exists in the Captains' scene in Shakespeare's *Henry V*; for when Fluellen generates with Macmorris the question of national identity, which focuses on his distinct and therefore separate national identity, the Irish captain responds, 'What ish my nation? Ish a villain, and a basterd, and a knave, and a rascal. What ish my nation? Who talks of my nation?' (III.ii.122–4). In this crucial passage, Macmorris throws the question back to Fluellen and thus aligns himself with The Covey; for both Irish characters argue that the manner in which we define a nation is arbitrary. Macmorris, then, appears to be telling Fluellen, 'Do not try to define us according to what you think we are' as a retort against those who attempt to define the Irish. Conversely, The Covey—a proponent of the proletariat—poses a definition that appears void of boundaries and therefore lacks an individualized identity as he resists labeling for the sake of national unity. Through this argumentative character, O'Casey—a member of the Citizen Army himself—uses socialism to rebut

---

[60]   Thomas Healy. 'Past and Present Shakespeares: Shakespearian Appropriations in Europe.' *Shakespeare and National Culture*. Ed. John J. Joughin. Manchester: Manchester UP, 1997. 217

[61]   The Irish Citizen Army formed in 1913 as a result of a massive strike of transport workers in Dublin. The ICA was founded by the Scottish-born James Connolly, a socialist, who fought for the protection of the workers. See Sean Farrell Moran's *Patrick Pearse and the Politics of Redemption: The Mind of the Easter Rising, 1916*. Washington, DC: Catholic University of America Press, 1994. 80–82.

nationalism; for the dramatist exposes the vainglorious leaders of the Irish Republic who remain trapped in the nation's mythic past and therefore promulgate a false heroism. Like Shakespeare, O'Casey questions the concept of national identity, and ultimately both playwrights show that a stable identification remains blurred as they question those who seek to perform the act of cultural delineation.

Arguably the most important section of *The Plough* appears in Act II; for here O'Casey seeks to establish the dichotomy between clerical and secular life in Ireland while at the same time elucidating how the blurring of religion and politics has occurred. In doing so, he appropriates several key scenes in *Henry V* which touch upon the same historiographical issues. While only the inside of a public house in downtown Dublin is visible to the audience in the opening scene, the speaker conducting the outside meeting of the Irish Citizen Army remains audible. Reacting to a slow night in her 'line' of work, Rosie, a prostitute, offers insight on the overall demeanor of the crowd outside: 'They're all in a holy mood. Th' solemn-lookin' dials on th' whole o' them an' they marchin' to th' meetin'. You'd think they were th' glorious company of th' saints, an' th' noble army of martyrs thramin' through th' streets of paradise' (162). Rosie's interpretation of the 'holy mood' of the men directly reflects the persuasion heard in the words of the orator at this public meeting. Before dissecting the rhetoric of the Speaker, we must recognize that O'Casey kept him nameless in the play for a reason. The Speaker in Act II represents Padraic Pearse, the highly revered Irish historical figure involved with inciting the common man to become soldiers and fight for freedom in the Easter Rising 1916. In fact, O'Casey borrowed segments of three of Pearse's writings for this Act: 'The Coming Revolution,' 'Peace and the Gael,' and a graveside oration for O'Donovan Rossa.[62] The Speaker in *Plough*, in place of the charismatic Pearse, equates the action of the Irish men going into battle to fight and shed their blood for Ireland's freedom with the utmost sacrifice—the crucifixion of Christ. Interestingly, his words echo Henry's famous speeches for his severely outnumbered soldiers, which we will examine here.

For the Irish Catholics, whose religion is planted deep within their culture, the Speaker's words ring loud and clear: 'Bloodshed is a cleansing and sanctifying thing, and the nation that regards it as the final horror has lost its manhood ... There are many things more horrible than bloodshed, and slavery is one of them!' (162).[63] The Speaker appeals to the Irishmen gathered in the town by reciting creeds taught by the Church, for the doctrine states that Christ's shedding of blood cleansed everyone born after His death and resurrection from sin, and therefore we are sanctified by His blood. Pearse also incited the group to overcome 'slavery' by English hands and join

---

[62]   Johnny Boyle also quotes from Pearse's graveside speech in *Juno and the Paycock*: 'Ireland only half free'll never be at peace while she has a son left to pull a trigger.' 27.

[63]   O'Casey quotes this passage from Pearse verbatim: 'Bloodshed is a cleansing and a sanctifying thing, and the nation which regards it as the final horror has lost its manhood. There are many things more horrible than bloodshed; and slavery is one of them.' From *Collected Works of Padraic Pearse: Political Writings and Speeches*. Dublin and London, 1922. 99.

the fight for emancipation. By appealing to their religious beliefs, the Speaker can be assured that these devout Christians will react to his words with the same zeal they might experience after a religious service or Mass.

The speaker's words reverberate with Henry's moving speech on the Feast of St Crispian:

> We few, we happy few, we band of brothers;
> For he to-day that sheds his blood with me
> Shall be my brother; be he ne'er so vile,
> this day shall gentle his condition;
> And gentlemen in England, now a-bed,
> Shall think themselves accurs'd they were not here;
> And hold their manhoods cheap whiles any speaks
> That fought with us upon Saint Crispian's day. (IV.iii.60–67)

Perhaps the greatest connection between the two plays which serve as a historical/ cultural critique is the emphasis on blood sacrifice and manhood. Earlier in *Henry V*, the young king discusses the necessity of bloodshed with the Bishop of Ely and the Archbishop of Canterbury. In this scene, Henry is depicted as a pre-lapserian figure in the first dialogue where the offending Adam has been whipped out of him:[64]

> Therefore take heed how you impawn our person,
> How you awake our sleeping sword of war—
> We charge you, in the name of God take heed;
> For never two such kingdoms did contend
> Without much fall of blood, whose guiltless drops
> Are every one a woe, a sore complaint,
> 'Gainst him whose wrongs gives edge unto the swords
> That makes such waste in brief mortality.
> Under this conjuration speak, my lord;
> For we will hear, note, and believe in heart,
> That what you speak is in your conscience wash'd
> As pure as sin with baptism. (I.ii.21–32)

Similarly, the Voice of the Speaker in *Plough* warns, 'War is a terrible thing, but war is not an evil thing … When war comes to Ireland she must welcome it as she would welcome the Angel of God!' (169). Like Henry, the Speaker is moralizing war and promotes it as a necessity for Ireland's freedom. In this context, both orators stress the need for war as well as the promise of a new time for their nations. However, Henry's speech is specious; he has no intention of achieving a sense of meritocracy through that action. There will not come to be a 'new time' in England where the status quo will be challenged. Also, Shakespeare presents Henry seriously

---

[64]   This refers to I.i. where Canterbury describes the king's transformation from Hal to Henry: 'Consideration like an angel came/and whipt th' offending Adam out of him'. 28–9.

on the eve before a great, nation-defining battle, whereas O'Casey seems to criticize as well as pervert Pearse's call to nationalism through the bar scene.[65]

If we contextualize these two speeches, the situations are historically quite similar; Pearse's group of volunteers lacked the skills of soldiers and were largely outnumbered by the Black and Tans, while Henry's forces were 'but a weak and sickly guard' (III.vi.155). On the eve of the Battle at Agincourt, the Chorus informs the audience 'The poor condemned English,/Like sacrifices, by their watchful fires/ Sit patiently and inly ruminate/The morning's danger' (IV.22–5). The audience senses the severity of the coming bloodbath in both the Irish and English plays and the unwavering intent of their resolute leaders. Relative to both plays' situations, we must remember that the English/French war is dominant versus dominant whereas the English/Irish struggle is dominant versus subordinate.

As the Speaker/Pearse continues his recitation in Act II of *Plough*, he sounds increasingly like a priest offering Mass: 'And we must be ready to pour out the same red wine in the same glorious sacrifice, for without the shedding of blood there is no redemption' (164). We may observe that clerical involvement in Irish politics was commonplace,[66] thus making the Speaker's role as 'priest' believable to the audience. The Speaker reminds them of Christ's crucifixion, which is considered a 'glorious sacrifice'; and if He had not suffered that horrendous death at Calvary, we would have 'no redemption.' The Speaker also refers to the sacrament of Holy Communion in this passage when he mentions the 'red wine.' Wine, used in Communion as a symbol of the blood Jesus shed for those who believe, serves to symbolize the blood of the Irish in this passage. By shedding their own blood for their nation, Ireland can be redeemed from the unwanted English authority that plagues them. Ironically, Fluther's actions inside the public house coincide with the mock Mass that is being celebrated by the Speaker, for the stage directions indicate that when he finishes his remarks which invoke Communion, Fluther is shown 'gulping down the drink that remains in his glass' (164). Peter also finishes his drink, and follows Fluther outside 'wiping his mouth with the back of his hand' (164). In this passage, Peter and Fluther, excited by the Speaker's words, react as they would if they are partaking in Communion in the Church. Upon drinking the wine, they return to the place they were standing in the midst of the Speaker. Thus, the bar serves as an altar, which reinforces the stereotype that the Irish find sanctity through intoxication. Despite the

[65]   The critic Raymond J. Porter posits that through the words of the Voice of the Man in *The Plough and the Stars*, 'O'Casey was prematurely debunking the "national myth" of the Easter Rising' and 'in the process he was ironically undercutting the very words of Pearse, a man who by his exemplary life and martyrdom for Irish freedom had been raised to the status of sainthood in the minds of Irish Catholic nationalists.' 'O'Casey and Pearse.' *Essays on Sean O'Casey's Autobiographies*. Ed. Robert G. Lowery. Totowa, NJ: Barnes and Noble, 1981. 90.

[66]   Pauric Travers. 'The Priest in Politics: The Case of Conscription.' *Irish Culture and Nationalism, 1750–1950*. Ed. Oliver MacDonagh, W.F. Mandler, and Pauric Travers. New York: St Martin's, 1983. 121.

somber nature of the historical event O'Casey portrays in this scene—and the play as a whole—this 'mock Communion' ceremony is quite comedic.

O'Casey uses Peter and Fluther to reflect the overall feelings of the crowd. Prior to their response to the sacrament of Holy Communion, the two men reveal the wave of excitement crashing over the group.

> *Fluther:* Jammed as I was in th' crowd, I listened to th' speeches pattherin' on th' peoples head, like rain fallin' on th' corn; every derogatory thought went out o' me mind, an' I said to meself, 'You can die now, Fluther, for you've seen th' shadow-dhreams of th' past leppin' to life in th' bodies of livin' men that show, if we were without a titther o' courage for centuries, we're vice versa now!' Looka here. *(He stretches out his arm under Peter's face and rolls up his sleeve.)* The blood was BOILIN' in me veins! (163)

Fluther's comments reiterate Pearse's own words of enthusiasm written in 'The Coming Revolution' in November 1913: 'The people itself will perhaps be its own Messiah, the people laboring, scourged, crowned with thorns, agonising and dying, to rise again immortal and impassable. For peoples are divine and are the only things that can properly be spoken of under figures drawn from the divine epos.'[67] Fluther takes the Speaker's (and Pearse's) challenge to be his own Messiah when he exposes his arms and reveals the blood boiling in his veins. Enticed and persuaded by the Speaker's crusade, Fluther speaks for all who are present when he comments on the courage bestowed on the Irish.

Similarly, in the opening of Act II of *Henry V*, the Chorus provides a striking image of the English soldiers as they wait to fight the French:

> Now all the youth of England are on fire,
> And silken dalliance in the wardrobe lies;
> Now thrive the armorers, and honor's thought
> Reigns solely in the breast of every man.
> They sell the pasture now to buy the horse,
> Following the mirror of all Christian kings,
> With winged heels, as English Mercuries.
> For now sits Expectation in the air,
> And hides a sword, from hilts unto the point,
> With crowns imperial, crowns and coronets,
> Promis'd to Harry and his followers. (II.1–11)

As with *Plough*, the working-class/common men who 'sell the pasture now to buy the horse' are represented in Henry V's militia. Given the resounding reaction by the unskilled soldiers in both *Henry V* and *Plough*—as assessed through the 'fire' that 'boils in their veins'—Colbert Kearney offers the following assessment:

> The speech succeeds because of the enormous prestige of this kind of rhetoric among those who have never learned it. Western civilisation began when skillful public speaking

---

[67]   In Padraic Pearse. *Collected Works.* 91–2.

was established as the art of rhetoric (*he rhetorike*) and this in turn developed into the study of language (*ars grammatica*) which was the basis of higher education and which distinguished the educated elite from the masses.[68]

Kearney recognizes that the speech is characterized by its 'literary' attributes, for it distinguishes the highbrow from the lowbrow, in this case the educated from those living in Dublin tenements.[69] When the Irish Volunteers prepare to march, O'Casey's stage directions indicate how the Speaker has won them over: '*They are in a state of emotional excitement. Their faces are flushed and their eyes sparkle; they speak rapidly, as if unaware of the meaning of what they said. They have been mesmerized by the fervency of the speeches*' (177). In addition to reflecting the success of the Speaker's rhetoric, O'Casey's description notes that the volunteers, filled with emotion, speak 'as if unaware of the meaning of what they said.' At the time this play was written, the Catholic Mass was delivered in Latin, a language only the educated could understand. Since the responses of those who attended Mass were also in Latin, many Catholics—especially if they were of the lower socio-economic class—would not have understood what they were actually saying. The stage directions which indicate the trance incited by the Speaker's call for action are comedic, and through this scene O'Casey indicts both the religious and political leaders who rally the populous who do not fully comprehend the ramifications of what they are being asked to do.

The 'Mass' concludes as the Citizen Army prepares to embark on their quest for freedom near the end of Act II. While Captain Brennan, Lieutenant Langon and Commandant Clitheroe ready themselves to march, they offer the following 'prayers' in sincere devotion:

> *Capt. Brennan (catching up The Plough and the Stars)*:
> Imprisonment for th' Independence of Ireland!
> *Lieut. Langon (catching up the Tri-colour)*: Wounds for th'
>   Independence of Ireland!
> *Clitheroe*: Death for th' Independence of Ireland!
> *The Three (together)*: So help us God! (178)

After the prayers, the Mass concludes with the exclamation, 'So help us God!', a response following prayer in the Catholic Church. Symbolically, Act II traces the Mass through the priest's sermon, the sacrament of communion, the response of the congregation and the prayer. It is in this context, then, that O'Casey illustrates how political ideology cannot operate separately from religion in the Irish nation state.

As we move to Act III, O'Casey reveals the impending chaos as the Easter Rising breaks. 'Language and culture once again run along parallel lines. One finds that the chaos of the language echoes the chaotic world of the characters.'[70] In fact,

---

[68]   Kearney. 'Sean O'Casey and the Glamour of Grammar.' 68.
[69]   Ibid.
[70]   Bernstein. 'What a Parrot Talks.' 271.

the language echoes the state of chaos evolving in the doomed city throughout the play as do the living conditions. Bernice Schrank sees the importance of the shift in language: 'While the changing circumstances impose new meanings on words, the characters' usage become cruder as the effects of the Rising are felt in the slum.'[71] The audience becomes aware of this shift at the onset of Act III, for the 'fine old Georgian house' (135) described in the opening of *Plough* evolves into

> a long, gaunt, five-story tenement; its brick front is chipped and scarred with age and neglect. The wide and heavy hall door, flanked by two pillars, has a look of having been charred by a fire in the distant past. The door lurches a little to one side, disjointed by the continual and reckless banging when it is being closed by most of the residents. The diamond-paned fanlight is destitute of a single pane, the framework alone remaining. The windows ... are grimy, and are draped with fluttering and soiled fragments of lace curtains.[72]

What was once playful banter between residents now becomes pessimism as Nora's uneasiness for her husband's safe return grows, bullets fly recklessly in the city streets, Peter is unwilling to help a disoriented woman who needs directions, and the bitter enemies Bessie Burgess and Mrs Gogan pair up to loot the abandoned stores lining Dublin's streets. The language again reflects the intensity of the chaos, for Captain Brennan yells 'Shut up, y' oul' hag!' to Bessie, who responds, 'Choke th' chicken, choke th' chicken, choke th' chicken!' (195). But perhaps the most severe illustration of the crashing wave of disorder is displayed when Jack snaps at his wife: 'Damn you, woman, will you let me go!' (197) He forces Nora away from him to rush back to battle, leaving her no tender words or intimations of hope. This cacophony of voices shows the failure of the Speaker's speech to incorporate the women into the fight. Afterwards, Fluther sums up the imminent chaos: 'The whole city can topple home to hell, for Fluther!' (198). As Shakespeare's Hamlet observes in his own forlorn environment, the time appears out of joint.

However, a more refined, more direct language is reflected in the characters' discourse in the fourth and final act of *The Plough and the Stars*, and this indicates the sense of order that comes of the dramatic tension. To begin with, Bessie's fiery manner quells as she keeps vigil over Nora, who loses her baby shortly after Jack dismisses her affections in the street. Also, we learn that Fluther, the same man who refused to help the disoriented woman in Act III find her way to Wrathmines, risks his life to make preparations for little Mollser's funeral. Mrs Gogan reveals, 'When all me own were afraid to put their noses out, you plunged like a good one through hummin' bullets, an' they knockin' fire out o' th' road, tinklin' through th' frightened windows, an' splashin' themselves to pieces on th' walls!' (209). Mollser, the dead child, necessitates a connection with Mary's unborn child in *Juno*, as O'Casey

---

[71] Bernice Schrank. '"There's Nothin' Derogatory in th' Use o' th' Word": A Study in the Use of Language in *The Plough and the Stars*.' *Irish University Review* 15.2 (1985): 174.
[72] Ibid. 180.

suggests that death and despair was born out of the uprising. In the beginning of *Plough*, the undisciplined language used by the characters contributes to the apparent chaos, but through their struggles, they become calm and gain eloquence.[73] The pervasive mood of chaotic disruption has been converted through the tragic situations in which the characters now find themselves.

Part of the disorder is exemplified through the tragic Nora, who evolves into an Ophelia-figure. Our first inclination of Nora's growing madness comes in Act III, when she reveals

> Th' agony I'm in since he left me has thrust away every rough thing he done, an' every unkind word he spoke; only th' blossoms that grew out of our lives are before me now; shakin' their colours before me face, an' breathin' their sweet scent on every thought springin' up in me mind, till, sometimes, Mrs. Gogan, sometimes I think I'm goin' mad! (186)

Sadly, Nora's transition from young newlywed to widow brings about a loss of reality. In Act IV,

> She is clad only in her nightdress; her hair, uncared for some days, is hanging in disorder over her shoulders. Her pale face looks paler still because of a vivid red spot on the tip of each cheek. Her eyes are glimmering with the light of incipient insanity; her hands are nervously fiddling with her nightgown. She halts at the door for a moment, looks vacantly around the room, and then comes slowly in. (204)

This depressing image of Nora Clitheroe is a far cry from O'Casey's depiction of her in Act I when she appears 'dressed in a tailor-made costume, and wears around her neck a silver fox fur' (147). Like the ill-fated Ophelia in Shakespeare's *Hamlet*, who, after learning of her father's murder by her lover appears 'distracted, with her hair down, playing on a lute' (IV.v), Nora's lack of rationality terrifies the people in her company. Nora serves as a vehicle in which O'Casey portrays the negativity associated with the cause of the Volunteers; for Nora's beloved Jack is more concerned with his responsibilities to the Citizen Army than with his young wife; and his disturbing declaration 'Ireland is greater than a wife' (178) at the end of Act II serves as a serious critique by the jaded dramatist.

Christopher Murray makes a distinction between the historical and moral elements of O'Casey's most controversial play:

> In the end, then, *The Plough* is not just a political play. It is certainly pacifist, a passionate protest against the violence sanctioned by Padraic Pearse. But it ... has to be seen, therefore, as a Shakespearean-style history play ... In Shakespeare, disorder and social confusion derive from some primal, moral evil, such as the killing of a king. In O'Casey, the disorder and social confusion derive from a mistaken corrective ... the politics, as

---

[73]   Ibid. 186.

in Shakespeare, are subservient to a vision of order which puts people before slogans or ideals.[74]

The breakdown of the system drives the narrative action that takes place in *Henry V* and O'Casey's *Juno* and *Plough*; for out of chaos derives order. Henry serves in the capacity of priest, like Pearse's Speaker does, for he follows the clergy's advice with his campaign of colonization and invokes the vengeful rhetoric of the Old Testament God before the war at Harfleur. Here, Shakespeare conveys the deceit embedded in Henry's language and also with organized religion. Similarly, O'Casey accomplishes this with the religious metaphors and symbolism that incite men to battle despite their own obvious disadvantaged state. Where apoliticism pervaded the first plays in each respective trilogy through the characters of Falstaff and Joxer, the final plays portray how the politics subside to an ordering that is achieved only through bloodshed.

Through plays grounded in historical events that unequivocally accentuate the national ideologies of their day, William Shakespeare and Sean O'Casey hold up mirrors to their respective cultures—albeit cynical. While O'Casey's allusions to Shakespeare's *Henriad* in terms of stylistics, characterizations and theme, and the ideological affinities have been discussed, one question still surfaces: why does O'Casey, an Irishman, appropriate the works of Shakespeare, an Englishman, to articulate his marginalized country's national identity?

At the conclusion of the opening act of *2 Henry IV*, the Archbishop of York eerily states, 'Past and to come seems best; things present worse' (I.iii.108). This forecast, although directed to England, reverberates throughout the Irish drama of Sean O'Casey. Clearly, a sense of trepidation permeates his plays as they reflect Irish culture. Although his dramas induced riots and protests, the portrayals of characters such as Juno, Captain Boyle, Joxer Daly, Fluther Good, The Covey, and Bessie Burgess mirrored Irish society amidst the backdrop of insurrection and his plays attempted to make sense of the 'state of chassis' that pervaded his Ireland. After the Dublin playwright's break with the Abbey, the Theatre's success diminished, and it was not until the Field Day Theatre Company opened its doors in 1980 in Northern Ireland that the Irish stage would enjoy international recognition once more.

---

[74]   Christopher Murray. 'The "Might of Design" in *The Plough and the Stars.' Irish Writers and Politics*. Ed. Okifumi Komesu and Masaru Sekine. Savage, MD: Barnes and Noble, 1990. 235.

Plates

Plate 1   Cover and poster, Field Day premiere of Translations. Painting by
           Basil Blackshaw

Plate 2   Field Day Theatre Company (left to Right):
Back Row: Ray McAnally, Rtephen Rea, Magdalena Rubalcava,
Liam Neeson, Bo Barton, Jonathan Tait, Shaun Scott.
Middle Row: Brian Friel, Mary Friel, Ann Hasson, Roy Hanlon,
Margo Harkin, Finola O'Doherty, Brenda Scanllon.
Front Row: Art O Briain, Mick Lally, Nuala Hayes, Paddy Woodworth,
David Heap. (Photo by Larry Doherty)

Plate 3   Brenda Scanllon as Bridget, Liam Neeson as Doalty in *Translations* by Brian Friel, Field Day Theatre Company. (Production photo by Rod Tuach.

Chapter 3

'Something is Being Eroded': Peripheral Visions in Contemporary Irish Drama

An investigation into the formation of the Field Day Theatre Company reveals how, in the tradition of the Abbey, Irish dramatists of the late twentieth century sought to establish a discourse separate from English hegemony. The political events in Northern Ireland following the Troubles[1] ultimately led to this push for cultural awareness in a location that had been excluded from the artistic and political mainstream. As such Field Day adopts an overt polypolitical agenda incorporating multiple voices representing an Ireland fragmented by geographical and ideological space. The company moves towards a broader spectrum of Irish literature with published pamphlets, *The Field Day Anthology of Irish Literature*, and creation of the 'fifth province'[2] to promulgate Irish intellectualism. Through these devices the Field Day depicted itself as a cultural entity distinct from England and the hegemony of Dublin.

Despite the overwhelming success of the Abbey Theatre in the early 1900s and the subsequent international popularity[3] of its premier plays—most notably J.M. Synge's *The Playboy of the Western World* and Sean O'Casey's *Juno and the Paycock* and *The Plough and the Stars*—Irish drama floundered in the years following O'Casey's highly acclaimed run in Dublin. This is not to suggest that new and well-received

---

[1]   The Troubles was a heightened period of military activity in Northern Ireland between English soldiers, the IRA, Protestants, and Catholics which spanned from the middle of the 1960s to the beginning of the 1980s.

[2]   The idea of a 'fifth province' was constructed by Richard Kearney and Mark Patrick Hederman, co-founders of journal *The Crane Bag*. As Christopher Morash notes, 'From the Field Day camp, the concept of an imaginary "Fifth Province" entered the Irish vocabulary, an imaginary place somewhere beyond (and yet inextricably part of) the historical four provinces of Ireland.' *A History of the Irish Theatre 1601–2000*. Cambridge: Cambridge UP, 2002. 256.

[3]   As Hugh Hunt chronicles, 'Grueling as the [American] tour was for the players as well as for Lady Gregory, it had dispelled for ever a falsely sentimental idea of Ireland and persuaded the intelligent American theatre-goers of the importance and vitality of the Irish theatre. For the future it was to make possible subsequent tours, and thereby provide the theatre with a much needed source of revenue. Through the developing interest of critics and public in Irish drama, playwrights ... have found a ready market for their plays both on and 'off' Broadway, while at home increasing numbers of American tourists have flocked to the Abbey Theatre.' *The Abbey*. 96.

plays were not staged during this period; indeed, playwrights like Brendan Behan and Hugh Leonard enjoyed success at home and across the globe. But the heyday of the Abbey and the Irish Renaissance seemed to be a distant memory for those committed to artistic production in Ireland. As a corollary, the quest for the nation's emergence as an independent culture appeared to subside for a time. The aftermath of the artistic success of the Irish Literary Revival left Ireland fixated on the glorious historical past of the early part of the century. Both political and literary figures, including Padraic Pearse, Michael Collins, William Butler Yeats, and James Joyce, remained alive in Ireland's memory. However, this national fixation for the past failed to generate a cultural response similar to that created by the Abbey, and as the century progressed and the Irish emigration decreased, the conceptualization of an active cultural ideology gave way to a poor economy, sprays of bullets, and the sound of bombs.[4] It was not until the 1970s that Ireland's identity crisis once again vaulted to the forefront of the political spectrum accompanied by a revitalization of artistic endeavor; in Ireland, politics and art speak to each other. Perhaps ironically, it was through a growing unrest following this acultural interval that the multi-faceted Irish question once again surfaced and efforts to coalesce North and the Republic mounted.

Where the main political struggles were seen in the capital city during the first three decades of the twentieth century, the tension now shifted to the religiously split North of Ireland in the latter thirty years. Both Belfast and Derry, or Londonderry, remain the sites of most of the internal strife at both the regional and national levels. Furthermore, two significant events that occurred in 1970s Derry became the impetus for international attention to focus on the growing problem in Northern Ireland. On Bloody Sunday, the first chief incident, thirteen civilians were shot to death by British soldiers during a protest on 30 January 1972 in Derry's bogside.[5] This atrocity sparked increased Irish Republican Army (IRA) activity especially in Northern Ireland, where already the economic and social conditions were deteriorating. The

---

[4]   Brian Fallon argues that while these years were seen as a transition period for Ireland—with Sean O'Casey leaving Dublin for England, the signing of the Peace Treaty, and the dismantling of the Abbey directorate—it was not necessarily a quiet time. But Fallon concedes that these thirty years were a 'transition from the Literary Revival dominated by Yeats ... and other founding fathers to a generation of writers which was largely self-contained and did not necessarily look to London as its centre; transition from a largely peasant society and the remnants of the Anglo-Irish Ascendancy to a country largely dominated by the newly emerging Catholic bourgeoisie; and politically, transition from dominion status inside the British Empire to a republic.' *An Age of Innocence: Irish Culture 1930–1960*. New York: St Martin's, 1998. 1.

[5]   'During a prohibited anti-internment rally in the city, British troops fired 108 live rounds in the Bogside, killing thirteen men ... The army claimed to have been shot at first, but there was scant evidence of this.' Marilyn J. Richtarik. *Acting Between the Lines: the Field Day Theatre Company and Irish Cultural Politics, 1980–1984*. Washington, DC: Catholic University of America Press, 2001. 21.

second major event which directly affected the citizens in Derry was the highly publicized hunger strike of Irish Republicans held in the Maze Prison which first began in 1980. Led by Bobby Sands, ten men perished as a result and two of them were Derry natives.[6] Outraged and disconcerted, both Protestants and Catholics in the North of Ireland felt helpless and underrepresented.

While these horrible incidents stand out in Irish history at the close of the twentieth century,[7] they were only two instances of the political strife that occurred during Ireland's Troubles. But as Jack Holland posits, 'The year of the hunger strike, 1981, was a turning point in more ways than one in the Ulster conflict. It was the last year in which more than 100 people lost their lives as a result of the political violence (101 died that year, including the 10 hunger strikers).'[8] With the heated violence appearing to subside, or at least diminish, the time was right for a communal effort to gain back some of what Northern Irish people lost during the recent years of bloodshed. Following the massacre on Bloody Sunday and the protest in the Maze Prison, Northern Ireland experienced a heightened awareness of nationalism.

'The end of art is peace':[9] The Field Day Theatre Company and the Culture of Resistance

It was against this strife-ridden backdrop in 1980 that the partnership of prominent Irish playwright Brian Friel, a Catholic from Derry, and actor Stephen Rea, a Protestant from Belfast, launched the Field Day Theatre Company. The establishment of this visionary theatre faction is important because of its desire to cross boundaries— literally and figuratively—by encompassing territories that had not been privy to this type of drama before. Unlike the Abbey Theatre, Field Day intended from the onset to reach out to the marginalized societies within Ireland. In fact, this artistic

---

    6   Richtarik contextualizes the situation: 'A new crisis had been reached in 1980, when Republican prisoners in the Maze Prison, who had been denied special category status after the end of internment in 1975, began a 'fast unto death' in support of their claim to be considered political prisoners. This protest was called off at New Year, but in March 1981 Bobby Sands began a new hunger strike campaign. He was joined at regular intervals by other hunger strikers, many of whom continued the fast after his death on 5 May. British Prime Minister Margaret Thatcher refused to consider their demands, and by the time the hunger strike ended in October ten prisoners had died' (68). This predicament caused a deeper rift between Ireland and England, and Bobby Sands emerged as a martyr for the Irish people.
    7   Bloody Sunday served as the basis of Brian Friel's *The Freedom of the City*, while the hunger strike inspired the Irish film, *Some Mother's Son*. In addition, both occurrences have bred a number of poems, folk ballads, and song lyrics, including the Irish rock band U2's hit, 'Sunday Bloody Sunday.'
    8   Jack Holland. *Hope Against History: The Course of Conflict in Northern Ireland.* New York: Henry Holt, 1999. 117.
    9   Seamus Heaney. 'The Haw Lantern.' *Selected Poems 1966–1987.* New York: The Noonday Press, 1995.

enterprise was distinctly different from typical companies, because the theatre group had no individual building to call their own. Their first production, the world premier of Brian Friel's highly acclaimed *Translations*, was staged in Derry's Guildhall. Also, no single director procured responsibility over the company; but rather a Board of Directors was instituted which consisted of six men from Northern Ireland. In addition to founders Friel and Rea, poets Seamus Heaney and Tom Paulin, literary critic Seamus Deane, and teacher David Hammond formed the original body. In an attempt to provide a sense of balance, three of the directors were Protestant and three were Catholic. Creating this symmetry between religious/political convictions was essential in helping the Field Day steer away from one monologist identity in Northern Ireland.

However, this parity has often been mistaken among critics as political neutrality. As Marilyn J. Richtarik states,

> The desire to avoid associating Field Day with any particular political position was especially marked in the beginning. It did seem necessary, however, to have some sort of general statement of purpose. This, in 1981, was kept very general and was much the same as it had been for *Translations*: 'firstly, to forge a Northern-based theatre company which would rehearse and tour in the North and then tour throughout the whole of Ireland; secondly, to concentrate on smaller venues, where theatre is rarely seen; and finally, to perform plays of excellence in a distinctively Irish voice that would be heard throughout the whole of the island.'[10]

Although a specific political affiliation was evaded, as the critic notes here, the Field Day did not feign the apoliticism of the Abbey. Rather, Field Day professes a polypoliticism which allowed the group to represent the various socio-cultural structures in Ireland. The insistence on stressing the 'Northerness' of the theatre is both interesting and applaudable.[11] Richtarik adds, 'Geography is crucial in this case'[12] in relation to the success of Field Day; this echoes the declaration of John Hume, Social and Democratic Labor Party (SDLP) leader, that the city of Derry is 'a microcosm of the Irish problem.'[13]

Richtarik also points out Field Day's endeavor to bring a highly politicized public space into rural communities with no typical access to theatre. The company was positioned to raise awareness of the Irish situation and shape a cultural rebellion. Whereas the urban/rural binary threatened the Anglo-Irish agenda of the Abbey Theatre, Field Day successfully incorporated the rural constituencies of Ireland in its touring program.

---

[10] Richtarik. *Acting Between the Lines*. 109.
[11] Derry was dealt a serious blow when, after promises of a new university opening to foster culture and create job security, the surveying team decided to build the institution elsewhere in Northern Ireland.
[12] Richtarik. *Acting Between the Lines*. 3.
[13] Frank Curran. *Derry: Countdown to Disaster*. Dublin: Gill, 1986. 1.

So why exactly would success bloom for a project of such magnitude in an area hard-hit with socioeconomic crisis and the free exchange of gunfire? According to co-director Seamus Heaney:

> We believed we could build something of value, a space in which we would try to redefine what being Irish meant in the context of what has happened in the North over the past 20 years, the relationship of Irish nationalism and culture. We were very conscious that we wanted to be quite independent of British influence exercised through Belfast and the equally strong cultural hegemony of Dublin.[14]

A predisposition for a unified national ideology resonates through Heaney's words and thus the underpinnings of the theatre. Heaney appears to suggest that Field Day wants to say what it means to be Irish from the Northern Irish position. The result of this desire to rediscover Irish identity in contemporary Ireland met with resounding applause in the early days of the theatre group; and for the first time after many years of exile[15] the literary figures and scholars who made up the Board of Directors felt as though they found their place once more in the North of Ireland.

Despite the theatre company's overt insistence on a position of polypoliticism, critics remained skeptical. Richtarik claims that Field Day did not promulgate 'a political "platform" partly because they want to be free to change their emphasis as circumstances and the general political climate change, and ... because they could not agree on a single political position among themselves.'[16] I believe, however, that this was a distinct benefit rather than a disadvantage. The avoidance of one, unified political view made the theatre company an asset to all socio-political divisions in Ireland. Field Day did not 'accept the North/South division, nor ignore the separate traditional strengths of those on either side.'[17] Therefore, Field Day sparked a pro-active response among a diverse set of directors, playwrights, and audiences across Ireland. Field Day's dialogic agenda encompassed the traditions of competing discourses in Ireland and explored the validity in each.

Benedict Anderson contends that the nation

> is imagined as a *community*, because, regardless of the actual inequality and exploitation that may prevail in each, the nation is always conceived as a deep, horizontal comradeship. Ultimately it is this fraternity that makes it possible, over the past two centuries, for so many millions of people, not so much to kill, as willingly to die for such limited imaginings.[18]

---

[14]   Quoted in Richtarik, *Acting Between the Lines*. 68.

[15]   Five out of the six directors left Northern Ireland and made their homes in either the Republic of Ireland or England.

[16]   Richtarik. *Acting Between the Lines*. 75.

[17]   Eric Binnie. 'Brecht and Friel: Some Irish Parallels.' *Modern Drama* 31 (1988): 366.

[18]   Benedict Anderson. *Imagined Communities: Reflections on the Origin and Spread of Nationalism*. London: Verso, 1991. 7.

Given Anderson's assertion, the community—whether it is metropolitan or agricultural—shares a kinship because of its similar convictions. In this case, the eclectic communities that make up Ireland, despite their differences, imagine themselves as a single nation. Field Day appears to share Anderson's ideology in their insistence on bridging binary oppositions and their attempt to raise national consciousness.

Field Day's nod towards tradition is closely linked with Ireland's history; of that rich historical past, the violence of imperial domination and, most importantly, of the quest for a national identity.[19] But Field Day has indeed incorporated broader concerns into their program, for following the success of Friel's *Translations*, Field Day's co-founder produced a version of Anton Chekhov's *Three Sisters*; in 1983 Athol Fugard's *Boesman and Lena* enjoyed a successful run; and Tom Paulin's *The Riot Act* appeared in 1984 as an adaptation of Sophocles's *Antigone* along with Derek Mahon's *High Time*, a version of Molière's *The School for Husbands*. Field Day attempts to bring global awareness home by re-staging Chekhov, Sophocles, and Molière in an Irish setting. In doing so, the company tries to achieve a parallel identity with these world dramatists. The reproductions engage the political debates of the original plays while reconstituting them so they speak to issues relevant to contemporary Ireland.

Richtarik asserts, 'Many of the people involved with Field Day reached political awareness during the 1960s ... Throughout the 1970s and 1980s, as people lost confidence in political action, the idea of culture as an alternative to politics gained ground.'[20] Thus the theatre becomes the place where a large group of people could gather together on common ground amidst the turbulence inherent in their society and foster a cultural rebellion.[21] We see a similar phenomenon coming from the Abbey; for the increasing violence and unrest of the early years of the twentieth century gave way to rioting during stage productions at Dublin's premier playhouse. The Playboy and Plough riots occur because of the discrepancy over how the Irish see themselves; and although they were understood as negative reactions by the audience, these representations of national identity on the Irish stage did serve as a form of cultural rebellion.

When asked the usual question regarding the genesis of Field Day, Seamus Deane proposes, 'Field Day "breaks new ground not in stage convention, not in theatrical language, but in the idea of breaking down the calcification of the theatrical audience." It was "inventing an audience".'[22] In a sense, by inventing an

---

[19]   For a critique of Field Day's enterprise, see Emelie Fitzgibbon, 'Theatre with its Sleeves Rolled Up.' *Irish Writers and Politics*. Ed. Okifumi Komesu and Masaru. Savage, MD: Barnes and Noble, 1990. 311.

[20]   Richtarik. *Acting Between the Lines*. 6.

[21]   A cultural rebellion serves as an alternative to political protest and thus fosters artistic venues that would raise national identity-consciousness. Incorporated in this idea is the redefinition of cultural values.

[22]   Quoted in Richtarik, *Acting Between the Lines*. 110.

audience, Field Day created a cultural ideology for the Northern Irish in particular. Consider, for example, Ernest Gellner's assertion, 'Nationalism is not the awakening of the nations to self-consciousness: it *invents* nations where they do not exist.'[23] Comparatively speaking, we can take the same position with the audience as Gellner does with nationalism; for Field Day composed an audience where one does not exist. Relative to Ireland, the geographical identity of the communities can only be reconstructed through creative invention. Field Day pro-actively promoted their own ideologies and trained the audience's receptivity to that dogma. Furthermore, the theatre company substitutes art and cultural awareness for the perpetuating turbulence this region has become so accustomed to.

This is one way in which the Field Day succeeded where the Abbey did not; for the Dublin stage catered to an Anglo-Irish audience whose primary concerns did not always include promoting an emergent national identity for Ireland. In fact, the Abbey audience's cultural awareness was quelled by the didacticism of the urban/ rural split in the theatre. But this is not to suggest that the Abbey had no effect on Field Day; for members of the Northern Ireland company were greatly influenced by Yeats and company. Friel's first play for the stage,[24] *The Enemy Within*, debuted at the Abbey, and Dublin's historical theatre had always served as a point of fascination for Rea. In fact, Rea was preoccupied with tales of the early Abbey Theatre and the Irish Renaissance. The actor reminisces, 'My ambition was to tour Ireland doing plays ... The original Abbey was an inevitable influence for me. What else can you name that had that total connection with what was going on around it? It was opening wounds.'[25] The Abbey was the first place where Rea auditioned after leaving the university, but he was greatly disillusioned; for he 'went consciously looking for the old Abbey, for the Irish nation. And of course it wasn't there.'[26] Perhaps Field Day attempted to pick up where the Abbey left off; certainly the Abbey was the seat of great Irish modern drama, and Field Day has added impressive components to contemporary Irish drama. As Rea describes:

I think Ireland's beginning to try and throw off the old colonial thing so that we can get on with it ourselves. In the end, you know, it's really up to the artists. They're often the only ones that can do it ... I think [the political situation is] desperate, and at the end of the day you can do very little about it. That's why I feel that Field Day is it for me. It's a political statement because we insist on being Northern, and we insist on being all Ireland as well, you see, so you can't get more political than that. And we believe that the energy of Ireland at this moment in time is coming from the North, and this is our expression of it.[27]

23 Fitzgibbon. 'Theatre with its Sleeves Rolled Up.' 169.
24 Friel wrote two radio plays before this.
25 Quoted in Richtarik, *Acting Between the Lines*. 84.
26 Ibid. 85.
27 Quoted in ibid. 86.

Rea's commentary alludes to the power of art—and drama in particular—as a vehicle for igniting and unifying a collective Irish identity. Rea's sentiments are echoed in Hammond's belief that 'it is time for Ireland to look toward the future.'[28] This remains a lofty enterprise, indeed, but Field Day's drama still looks to its past to combat present-day and future enemies.

Three veins of looking ahead for Field Day, in addition to the annual dramatic productions, were developed within the first decade of the company, and each met with criticism. First, the Board of Directors decided to publish three pamphlets approximately every six months that would address major issues in Irish nationalism, politics, and culture. While the first installment appeared in 1983, the collection *Nationalism, Colonialism, and Literature* published in 1990 by Terry Eagleton, Frederic Jameson, and Edward Said stands apart from the rest. In the introduction of the text, Seamus Deane affirms, 'Ireland is the only Western European country that has had both an early and a late colonial experience ... Irish writing ... has once more raised the question of how the individual subject can be envisaged in relation to its community, its past history, and a possible future.'[29] The truth of Deane's assertion is often overlooked; because, until recently, people generally have not associated Ireland with the plight of Third World countries, for example, in similar late colonial experiences.

Clearly, the pamphlets intended to discuss postcolonial issues more directly than the plays would be able to. Deane adds that the goal of the pamphlets was to 'address ... with some force and brevity' rhetorics of coercion and liberation 'in relation to the present northern and Anglo-Irish situation.'[30] Once again we see an effort to cross border lines between Northern Ireland and the Republic. However, I argue that the pamphlets ultimately remove an agency from the audience itself by assuming that all Irish people will react to the publications the same way. In particular, I am skeptical with regards to the accessibility of these pamphlets and the target audience. Scholars may certainly benefit from the writings, but I seriously doubt whether the working class to which O'Casey appealed would have had access to this kind of text.

The second non-dramatic avenue by Field Day was the development of the 'fifth province,' which David Cairns and Shaun Richards define as 'the location of the critical alliance of many Irish artists and intellectuals—North and South—whose involvement with both Field Day and *The Crane Bag*[31] suggests that the detached yet concerned critical examination of the roots of the present crisis can be made a

---

[28]   Quoted in ibid. 103.

[29]   Seamus Deane. *Nationalism, Colonialism, and Literature.* Ed. Terry Eagleton, Frederic Jameson, and Edward W. Said. Minneapolis: University of Minnesota Press, 1990. 3–4.

[30]   Deane. *Nationalism, Colonialism, and Literature.* 14.

[31]   As explicated by Cairns and Richard in *Writing Ireland, The Crane Bag* was 'a cultural/literary/political journal whose short-lived career was dedicated to the creation of 'the neutral ground where things detach themselves from all partisan and prejudiced connection and show themselves for what they really are.' 149.

reality.'[32] Undeniably, this is an essential addition to the Irish intellectual landscape as it promised to 'create a shared context which might make possible communication across Ireland's border.'[33] Once again the politicizing of the Irish question remained prominent but neutral in terms of identifying with one party platform. This idea of a 'fifth province' offered cultural exile, in some respects, to those individuals caught up in the crossroads between Northern Ireland and the Republic.

Thirdly, the theatre company published an anthology of Irish writings, an idea which stemmed from Deane's selection in the second group of pamphlets. Deane proposes,

> One step towards that dissolution [of the mystique of Irishness] would be the revision of our prevailing idea of what it is that constitutes the Irish reality. In literature that could take the form of a definition, in the form of a comprehensive anthology, of what writing in this country has been for the last 300–500 years. … Everything, including our politics and our literature, has to be rewritten—i.e., re-read. That will enable new writing, new politics, unblemished by Irishness, but securely Irish.[34]

This became the incentive for the *Field Day Anthology of Irish Writing*, a multi-volume collection of literary, philosophical, social, political and scientific texts. While the first installments (1991) received harsh criticism, especially from women who felt underrepresented,[35] the anthology serves as an important resource for scholars in a variety of disciplines; without the intervention of Field Day, a text of this magnitude might never have been published.[36] Certainly, this motivation resonates with similar ideology expressed by both the Abbey and Field Day agendas on the dramatic front. It is imperative for Ireland to define itself by those facets that make it different— and by different, independent—from England. But the 'principles of hierarchy and exclusion' that Deane professes are inevitable with such an undertaking open Field Day's efforts up for a harsh backlash.[37] But one problem the anthology does address

[32]   Cairns and Richard. *Writing Ireland*. 149.

[33]   Binnie. 'Brecht and Friel.' 366.

[34]   Seamus Deane. 'Heroic Styles: The Tradition of an Idea.' *Ireland's Field Day*. London: Field Day Theatre Company, 1985. 58.

[35]   This issue was recently rectified—to some extent—with the publication of *The Field Day Anthology of Irish Writing: Irish Women's Writing and Traditions*. Ed. Angela Bourke, Siobhan Kilfeather, Maria Luddy, et al. Cork: Cork UP, 2002.

[36]   In his introduction to *Nationalism, Colonialism, and Literature*, Deane makes it clear that the purpose of the anthology 'is not to establish a canon as such; it is to engage in the action of establishing a system that has an enabling, a mobilizing energy, the energy of assertion and difference, while remaining aware that all such systems—like anthologies of other national literature—are fictions that have inscribed within them principles of hierarchy and of exclusion, as well as inclusion, that become evident only when the mass of material is organized into a particular form.' 15.

[37]   Evelyn Toynton attacks Field Day for glossing over the 'effect' and focusing instead solely on the 'cause' of Irish oppression: 'In their dogged insistence on placing everything in

along these lines is the idea that Irish writers have essentially been categorized as 'British.' Because of this impropriety, numerous writers and their creative works were overlooked primarily because they were not popular in England. As we can see, Irish writers have largely been doubly marginalized and misrepresented.

This three-pronged agenda of the Field Day Theatre Company—to produce pamphlets with nationalist themes, encourage a 'fifth province' free of borders where intellectuals can work together, and publish extensive anthologies of Irish writings—may appear to serve only the Irish intelligentsia. The pamphlet collections discuss issues such as imperialism, politics, cultural identity, and so on. While these writings certainly pertain to the Irish people, the accessibility of these scholarly tracts is questionable—especially for people living in rural areas. In addition, the 'fifth province' directly targets intellectuals, and thus leaves no room for the common Irish citizen. Also, the multi-volume anthology originally sold for $150.00 in the US, hardly an affordable price. Therefore, it is most likely to be found in libraries—academic libraries, that is. In sum, it appears that all of these agendas founded by Field Day appeal to academicians. However, I believe that Field Day's objective is to establish an Irish intelligentsia separate and distinct from England, and this is a rather cogent venture. Once again, Irish writers have long been covered under the umbrella of 'British'; this is most obvious in the inclusion of select Irish literary figures in British anthologies. The benefits of this innovative endeavor can be seen at the present time with the heightened awareness of the Irish colonial condition in addition to an increased consciousness of modern and *contemporary*[38] Irish writers.

Consequently, the Field Day Theatre Company has been successful to varying degrees in first establishing a dramatic oeuvre especially in, but not exclusively to, Northern Ireland. Second, the enterprise's goal in promoting an emergent Irish intellectualism that is another important way to define the nation's independence from the pervasive hegemonic culture that still attempts to assimilate it. A new project has surfaced more recently that intends to serve the linguistic ends of the Irish question and, at the same time, benefit the majority of the people. As F.C. McGrath explains,

> Field Day proposes to appropriate the English language for the Irish by identifying and promoting a distinct form of Irish English, distinct in the sense of possessing unique words, syntactical forms, idioms, and spoken rhythms that do not characterize the language in

---

a certain kind of political context, they seem to reduce historical acts and developments to mere mental phenomena, so that the political content here is in fact robbed of much force and urgency.' 'Themselves.' *The American Scholar* 62 (1993): 284.

[38]   I emphasize the contemporary Irish writers because it is time for scholarship to examine the rich writings of late twentieth- and early twenty-first-century literary figures of this marginalized nation. For too long, the critical attention has been placed primarily on Joyce, Yeats, and Shaw. While the genius of these writers is not contested here, there are numerous male and female Irish writers who also deserve consideration.

other English-speaking nations. To advance this notion of Irish English, Field Day has proposed the compilation of an Anglo-Irish dictionary.[39]

Field Day's motive in assembling an Anglo-Irish dictionary would be to instigate a reverse linguistic assimilation—that is, to incorporate the very language that originally stripped away the Gaelic tongue from the Irish culture.

Since the onset of Field Day, a split has occurred within the Board of Directors, a division caused, according to Richtarik, by the 'fault line between art and criticism … the Field Day plays and the Field Day pamphlets, but it was also evident in statements by the directors, in interviews and programme notes, about the company.'[40] This split between criticism and art—the two cultural binaries which feed into the Field Day's main objectives—may ultimately divide the company into separate entities. But despite its difficulties, Field Day is still producing critical texts and gaining national—and international—attention. No doubt, Stephen Rea's successful career has helped garner attention for his theatre company. Friel resigned from the Board of Directors after the first ten years, but his plays are enjoying renewed success in theatres all over the world and have been adapted for the cinema. Another success story from the North of Ireland was gained for poet Seamus Heaney, who was awarded the Nobel Prize for Literature in 1996. But each founder of Field Day, through his individual struggles and successes, has helped in re-creating an emergent national culture for Ireland.

As Frantz Fanon reminds us, 'A national culture is not a folk-lore, nor an abstract populism that believes it can discover a people's true nature. A national culture is the whole body of efforts made by a people in the sphere of thought to describe, justify and praise the action through which that people has created itself and keeps itself in existence.'[41] Therefore, the combination of efforts forged by Field Day—the plays, pamphlets, 'fifth province,' and anthologies—have not only ignited but have perpetuated Ireland's national culture as well as her emerging identity. This is more significant since the location of this cultural thrust, Northern Ireland, has long been faced with marginalization within its own nation. Not only are the Northern natives peripherized and denigrated as the Other by England—the dominant imperial order in that territory—but they are also considered peripheral to the Republic of Ireland. Also, across border lines, the North remains the objectified domain because of the presence of the English. Moreover, the Republic is home to Dublin, the Irish metropolis and the seat of political, economic, and intellectual authority, whereas Northern Ireland's forlorn cities are home to a poor economy and violence. Finally, Protestants of the North are still stereotyped by the Catholic minority, which is, in turn, stigmatized by the Protestant majority. Therefore, the English/Northern, Republic/

[39] F.C. McGrath. *Brian Friel's (Post)Colonial Drama: Language, Illusion, and Politics.* Syracuse: Syracuse UP, 1999. 203.

[40] Richtarik. *Acting Between the Lines.* 239.

[41] Frantz Fanon. 'On National Culture.' *The Post-Colonial Studies Reader.* Ed. Bill Ashcroft, Gareth Griffiths, and Helen Tiffin. London: Routledge, 1995. 153.

Northern, and Protestant/Catholic dichotomies reflect this manifold oppression. Ireland's national identity is so intertwined with England that it is impossible not to mention the struggles the Irish face under the oppression of English colonialism. However, what seems like a bleak existence for the Northern Irish has made them stronger; as long as there is revolution in the theatre, and companies like the Abbey and Field Day to forge a culture of resistance, no portion of Ireland will succumb to the suffocating web of imperial domination.

Colonial Domination and Deculturation in Brian Friel's *Translations* and Shakespeare's *Henriad*

In *Black Skin, White Masks*, Frantz Fanon claims 'A man who has a language consequently possesses the world expressed and implied by that language ... Mastery of language affords remarkable power.'[42] Certainly, this ideology can be traced through the study of thousands of years of linguistics, and in direct relation to this study, as the cause and effect of imperial domination by one people over another. Moreover, Fanon continues, 'Every colonized people—in other words, every people in whose soul an inferiority complex has been created by the death and burial of its local cultural originality—finds itself face to face with the language of the civilizing nation; that is, with the culture of the mother country.'[43] This involuntary deculturation by a hegemonic force surfaces as an underlying theme in contemporary Irish playwright Brian Friel's powerful play *Translations*, the inaugural production of the Field Day Theatre Company in Northern Ireland in the fall of 1980. In this dramatic interpretation of the conflict brought about by the Ordnance Survey, Friel masterfully creates a bridge between the Gaelic-speaking residents of Baile Baeg in 1833 pre-famine Ireland and the Northern Ireland audience whose culture and individual identity have been saturated with similar issues of erosion; for, as the play articulates—and as the present-day audience is brutally aware—the Irish people have suffered an erosion on linguistic, political and cultural levels. As Nicholas Grene explains, 'This is, in one sense, a text in which the empire writes back, an Irish playwright uses the English language to commemorate the Irish culture of which the English colonists deprived him and his.[44] Friel's play depicts how England exerted blatant political hegemony over her territory and then elucidates the horrific effects of this cultural usurpation on the eager students at Hugh O'Donnell's hedge school.[45]

---

[42]   Frantz Fanon. *Black Skin, White Masks*. New York: Grove Press, 1967. 18.

[43]   Ibid.

[44]   Nicholas Grene. *The Politics of Irish Drama: Plays in Context from Boucicault to Friel*. Cambridge: Cambridge UP, 1999. 47.

[45]   Hedge schools were unofficial schools with an informal approach to education and were run by individual scholars. According to P.J. Dowling in *The Hedge Schools of Ireland* (Cork: Mercier Press, 1968)—which Friel used as a source for *Translations*—'The beginnings

According to S.J. Connolly, 'In contemporary Northern Ireland, culture remains a live political issue.'[46] More importantly, politics remain a live cultural issue; for the literature coming out of the North since Bloody Sunday remains entrenched in political ideology as the historiographical re-centering of marginalized voices. Whether or not the intent of contemporary Irish literature is to promulgate political activism or a subtle awareness of the issues at hand, the union of politics and art is inescapable for the poets, fiction writers and film directors from Northern Ireland. Consequently, culture (art) informs the political spectrum, and vice versa. Edward Said offers an interesting observation relative to this point: 'Reading and interpreting the major metropolitan cultural texts in this newly activated, re-informed way could not have been possible without the movements of resistance that occurred everywhere in the peripheries against the empire.'[47] As a component of one of the 'movements of resistance' then, it is not surprising that Friel's play not only utilizes classical allusions of ancient Greece and Rome but appropriates Shakespeare's *Henriad* in the postcolonial-minded *Translations* with the intent of showing how Shakespeare can be read in relation to a Celtic Other.

Although this appropriation has been intelligently addressed in Anthony Roche's essay, 'A Bit Off the Map: Brian Friel's *Translations* and Shakespeare's *Henry IV*,'[48] the relationship between Shakespeare's *1 Henry IV* and *Translations* is more complex than mere allusions between the mapmaking scene in III.i. with the Royal Engineers'[49] topographical employment, and the love scene between Mortimer and his Welsh wife as comparable with the climactic kiss between Maire and Yolland.

---

of the Hedge School date back to the 17th century. The "Popish Schoole Masrs." mentioned in the Cromwellian Records who taught "the Irish youth, trayning them up in Supersticion, Idolatry, and the Evil Customs of the Nacion" were probably the first hedge schoolmasters ... Because the law forbade the schoolmaster to teach, he was compelled to give instruction secretly: because the householder was penalised for harbouring the schoolmaster, he had perforce to teach, and that only when the weather permitted, out of doors' (35).

[46]   S.J. Connolly. 'Culture, Identity and Tradition: Changing Definitions of Irishness.' *In Search of Ireland: A Cultural Geography*. Ed. Brian Graham. London: Routledge, 1997. 43.

[47]   Said. *Culture and Imperialism*. 53.

[48]   *Literary Interrelations: Ireland, England and the World—II: Comparison and Impact*. Ed. Wolfgang Zach (intro.) and Heinz Kosok. Tubingen: Narr, 1987.While Roche's article is informative and draws parallels between the two plays, by focusing on *1 Henry IV*, this study fails to engage the deeper connections with *2 Henry IV* and especially *Henry V*. Also, while Roche argues that Friel's play is 'a response—linguistic, political, cultural, but above all dramatic—to the issues raised in and by [III.i.],' I argue that *Translations* is not merely a response but a gaelicizing of the issues which surface in Shakespeare's *Henriad*.

[49]   For example, Brabantio indicts Othello—another representative of the Other—for using witchcraft as a method of obtaining Desdemona's affections: 'Damned as thou art, thou hast enchanted her' (I.ii.63) ... 'Thou hast practic'd on her with foul charms' (73). Brabantio raises further accusations because he is positive that 'She is ... corrupted/By spells and medicines bought of mountebanks;/For nature so prepost-rously to err ... Sans witchcraft could not' (I.iii.60-4).

While critics have, to some degree, discussed the issue of language in Friel's play, no one has addressed the deeper implications of the linguistic parallels with the entire *Henriad*. In particular, while these two scenes that Roche mentions are significant, *2 Henry IV* is also appropriated by Friel in terms of the topic of the erosion of language, while *Henry V* becomes a crucial text for Friel regarding the linguistic conquest of the French princess Katherine and treatment of the Others—Macmorris, Fluellen, and Jamy—in terms of the construction of identity. Collectively these plays offer a critique of colonialism's agenda and expose the effects of dispossession and deculturation on marginalized peoples.

Thematically, the complications with the construction and destruction of identity are depicted in this text. Said explains,

> The construction of identity ... involves the construction of opposites and 'others' whose actuality is always subject to the continuous interpretation and re-interpretation of their differences from 'us.' Each age and society re-creates its 'Others.' Far from a static thing then, identity of self or of 'other' is a much worked-over historical, social, intellectual, and political process that takes place as a contest involving individuals and institutions in all societies.[50]

In the opening act of Shakespeare's *1 Henry IV*, we see the manifestation of Said's assertion, for Westmerland calls the Welshman Owen Glendower 'irregular and wild' (I.i.40) and comments on 'the rude hand of that Welshman' (I.i.41); while Worcester refers to him as 'that great magician, damn'd Glendower' (I.iii.83). Glendower, in direct opposition to the King's forces, is stereotyped by his nemesis as barbarous and exotic/magical—the typical stigmatisms placed on colonized peoples.[51] This typecasting feeds the ensuing alienation of the oppressed and what Homi Bhabha indicts as 'those terrifying stereotypes of savagery, cannibalism, lust and anarchy which are the signal points of identification and alienation, scenes of fear and desire, in colonial texts.'[52] Thus, Westmerland and Worcester intend for the Welsh rebel to be taken less seriously or rationally. From the onset, then, the Welsh/Celtic characters are denigrated for their Otherness by England's dominant social order and therefore placed in the 'object' category—a facet of colonization that will resurface again in *Henry V*.

While Shakespeare does in fact articulate the issue of barbarity in *1 Henry IV*, he indicts the English. As Roche recognizes, 'The one jangling, dissonant presence is ... Harry Percy, who fully earns his nickname "Hotspur" by threatening the delicate political negotiations with his short temper and outspoken views.'[53] Shakespeare portrays Hotspur's antagonism with the others most poignantly in the map scene—a junction in the play that illustrates a form of deterritorialization. Roche further notes

---

[50]   Edward Said. *Orientalism*. New York: Vintage. 332.
[51]   Ibid.
[52]   Bhabha. *The Location of Culture*. 72.
[53]   Roche. 'A Bit Off the Map.' 140.

that the map serves as the signifier of 'two antagonistic world views'[54] between the two men in terms of their different readings of its representation. In III.i.69–70, Glendower initiates the mapping issue: 'Come, here is the map. Shall we divide our right/According to our threefold order ta'en?' There is no evidence to suggest that the Welshman attempts to cheat Hotspur out of his share; in fact, Mortimer agrees that 'The Archdeacon hath divided it/Into three limits very equally' (71–2) and continues to explicate the divisions. As the men make plans to stall the rebellion, Hotspur appears contrary and argumentative:

Methinks my moi'ty, north from Burton here,
In quantity equals not one of yours.
See how this river comes me cranking in,
And cuts me from the best of all my land
A huge half-moon, a monstrous [cantle] out.
I'll have the current in this place damm'd up.
And here the smug and silver Trent shall run
In a new channel fair and evenly.
It shall not wind with such a deep indent,
To rob me of so rich a bottom here. (III.i.95–104)

However, Hotspur's ideas of how the map should be drawn cheats Glendower and Mortimer out of their equal portion of the land, and Mortimer brings this fact to light. What follows this satirical representation of colonial greed is a stubborn quarrel between Glendower and Harry Percy:

Hot: I'll have it so, a little charge will do it.
Glend: I'll not have it alt'red.
Hot: Will not you?
Glend: No, nor you shall not.
Hot: Who shall say me nay?
Glend: Why, that will I.
Hot: Let me not understand you then,
Speak it in Welsh. (III.i.114–18)

Aside from his obstinacy in the matter of equal division of the land, Hotspur again relegates Glendower in the category of the Other through his linguistic game. By referring to Glendower's language with an air of dismissal, Hotspur creates social/caste categories. On the other hand, Hotspur, representative of the English stereotype, displays complete ignorance in this section, and Glendower adds his own insult:

[54]   Ibid.

> I can speak English, lord, as well as you,
> for I was train'd up in the English court,
> Where being but young I framed to the harp
> Many an English ditty lovely well,
> And gave the tongue a helpful ornament,
> A virtue that was never seen in you. (III.i.119–24)

Here Glendower asserts his linguistic capabilities versus Harry Percy's unsophisticated courtier capacities as a means of rebuttal. In doing so, Shakespeare elucidates not only the English's narrow-mindedness and imposition upon the Celtic culture, but also the bilingual capabilities of the Celtic people. This issue is picked up by Friel primarily through Jimmy Jack, called 'The Infant Prodigy' because of his ability to quote Greek and Latin, and the other Gaelic-speaking students at the hedge school.

The boundaries of the distinct cultures come into the forefront with the visitation of the Lady Hotspur and Mortimer's wife, who is also Glendower's daughter. Mortimer laments: 'This is the deadly spite that angers me: /My wife can speak no English, I no Welsh' (III.i.190–91). Therefore, his father-in-law must 'translate' for his daughter, who only speaks her native tongue. The stage directions indicate *'Glendower speaks to her in Welsh, and she answers him in the same'*; and a little further in the passage Mortimer responds

> I understand thy looks. That pretty Welsh
> Which thou pourest down from these swelling heavens
> I am too perfect in, and but for shame,
> In such a parley should I answer thee.
> > *The lady again in Welsh.*
> I understand thy kisses, and thou mine,
> And that's a feeling disputation,
> But I will never be a truant, love,
> Till I have learn'd thy language, for thy tongue
> Makes Welsh as sweet as ditties highly penn'd,
> Sung by a fair queen in a summer's bow'r,
> With ravishing division, to her lute. (198–208)

This scene reveals a communication separate from linguistics, for some level of mutual understanding is achieved. But what is most interesting is Mortimer's desire to learn the language of the colonized and his wish to be assimilated into the culture of the Other. When his wife speaks once more in Welsh, he is exasperated and chides, 'O, I am ignorance itself in this!' (III.i.210). But the real ignorance surfaces through Hotspur, for when Mortimer's wife desires an audience for her singing, consider Lady Hotspur's reaction to her husband's insolent behavior:

Hot: Now I perceive the devil understands Welsh
       And 'tis no marvel he is so humorous.
       By'r lady, he is a good musician.
Lady P: Then should you be nothing but musical,
         for you are altogether govern'd by humors. Lie still,
         ye thief, and hear the lady sing in Welsh.
Hot: I had rather hear Lady, my brach, howl in Irish.
Lady P: Wouldst thou have thy head broken?
Hot: No.
Lady P: Then be still.
Hot: Neither, 'tis a woman's fault.
Lady P: Now God help thee!
Hot: To the Welsh lady's bed. (III.i.229–42)

This playful banter reveals that, while Mortimer strives to achieve acculturation, Hotspur clearly subscribes to deculturation. He is an Englishman who clearly accedes to a xenophobic agenda and shares no interest in Other cultures or identities beside his own. Furthermore, the sexual innuendo at the end of this passage reflects the language of the oppressor, for Hotspur views the Welshwoman in sexual terms. Michael Cronin adds,

> Mortimer's earnest entreaty … contrasts with Hotspur's mocking association of Welsh music with the diabolic … For Mortimer, the language of the Celtic other is a source of curiosity, enchantment and sentiment. It is euphonic and seductive. For Hotspur, the speech of the Celtic other is harsh and uninteresting, the butt of a joke rather than an invitation to learn.[55]

The tender love scene collapses into the mapmaking scene of III.i., but the primary purpose of this segment of the play, the aestheticization of the Other, is reiterated when, prior to the lady's song, Mortimer states 'With all my heart I'll sit and hear her sing./By that time will our book, I think, be drawn' (III.i.220–21); and at the close of the scene, Glendower reveals 'By this our book is drawn, we'll but seal,/And then to the horse immediately' (265–6). Thus, the primary concern of the men is not their wives but the completion of the map; the wives are, metaphorically, maps already drawn.

Also, there is a distinct parallel between this scene and Henry's 'courting' of Katherine in *Henry V*. While the English monarch's colonizing discourse has been discussed at length in Chapter 1, additional elements of V.ii. must be addressed with regard to the demonizing/sexualizing of the conquered Other. For example, as Henry and Katherine finish their linguistically challenged courtship, they kiss. Henry responds, 'You have witchcraft in/your lips, Kate' (V.ii.275–6). We must keep

---

[55] Michael Cronin. 'Rug-headed kerns speaking tongues: Shakespeare, Translation and the Irish Language.' *Shakespeare and Ireland: History, Politics, Culture*. Ed. Mark Thornton Burnett and Ramona Way. New York: St Martin's, 1997. 200–1.

in mind that although France is a powerful, Western nation, England's desire is to assert colonial domination over her; therefore, in casting France/Katherine in the category of the Other, the nation/princess is objectified and the imperial process is manifested. Directly following the kiss, the courtiers enter the scene and inquire into the process of the final phase of Henry's conquest. The English monarch replies,

> Our tongue is rough, coz, and my condi-
> tion is not smooth; so that having neither the voice nor
> the heart of flattery about me, I cannot so conjure up
> the spirit of love in her, that he will appear in his true
> likeness. (286–90).

This passage indicates additional references to Katherine and witchcraft; and the colonizer fails to 'conjure up the spirit' because he does not fit into the supernatural stereotypes of the Other. Therefore, Katherine is identified with the 'magician' Glendower, for they are both marginalized and denigrated as a result of their foreignness to the oppressor.

What I have found particularly interesting in terms of this study in the components of Shakespeare's *Henriad* is the linguistic progression and fulfillment of the colonization process. To be more specific, in *1 Henry IV*, the construction of the map and the equal division of land lies at the forefront of III.i., but in *2 Henry IV*, the discourse becomes much more precise in terms of the imperial mission. For example, Lord Bardolph explains:

> When we mean to build,
> We first survey the plot, then draw the model,
> And we see the figure of the house,
> Then must we rate the cost of the erection ...
> Much more, in this great work
> (Which is, almost, to pluck a kingdom down
> And set another up), should we survey
> The plot of situation and the model,
> Consent upon a sure foundation,
> Question surveyors, know our own estate. (I.iii.41–4, 48–53)

Bardolph provides us with a distinct colonizing discourse that uses proprietary language metaphorically to construct imperial domination over other territories. Finally, in *Henry V*, assimilation is completed through the conquest of the French crown—and through the subjugation of Katherine. However, the colonizing discourse appears the strongest in this final play and the ramifications are much more severe. Those who will suffer imperial domination face the fear of eviction and dispossession—just like Friel's Irish characters do. Finally, what is most prominent in these three plays is England's constant attempt to colonize a Western Other.

The Irish Erasure: Assimilation and Colonization of the Other

In his 'Afterword' added in the 1994 edition of *Orientalism*, Said writes:

> What I called for in *Orientalism* was a new way of conceiving the separations and conflicts that had stimulated generations of hostility, war, and imperial control. And indeed, one of the most interesting developments in post-colonial studies was a re-reading of the canonical cultural works, not to demote or somehow dish dirt on them, but to re-investigate some of their assumptions, going beyond the stifling hold on them of some version of the master-slave binary dialectic ...[56]

The richness of this text stems from its conceptualization of the Subject/Object relationship and the components of the Center/Periphery of our literary and historical past. The critic refers to some recent texts and groups of resistance 'whose daring new formal achievements are in effect a re-appropriation of the historical experience of colonialism, revitalized and transformed into a new aesthetic of sharing and often transcendent re-formulation.'[57] One such collective is Ireland's Field Day Theatre Company, whose primary goal remains to re-conceptualize 'historical experiences which had once been based on the geographical separation of peoples and cultures'[58] as a result of colonization.

At the forefront of this reformulation in contemporary Northern Ireland is Friel's *Translations*; for it refashions Shakespeare's concepts dealing with the inherent difficulties of linguistic, political, and cultural issues of colonial intervention and gaelicizes these issues. The play opens with a scene between Manus, the disabled son of the hedge schoolmaster—who is a fine scholar and teacher himself—and Sarah, a mute student described as having a speech defect so severe *'that all her life she has been considered locally to be dumb and she has accepted this: when she wishes to communicate, she grunts and makes unintelligible nasal sounds'* (383). Interestingly, then, *Translations* begins with a scene of fractured discourse and an absence of narrative; when Sarah finally speaks the phrase 'My name is Sarah' (384), Manus revels 'Now we're really started! Nothing'll stop us now! Nothing in the wide world!' and further notes, 'soon you'll be telling me all the secrets that have been in that head of yours all these years' (385). Manus's discourse reveals both the importance of effective communication and the power of language in constructing one's identity.

In essence, Manus teaches Sarah that speaking, i.e., articulating her language, can allow her to tell her own history; a gift that will thus yield empowerment via the creation of her own narrative. Roche offers a similar view on this scene and affords a connection between Hotspur's preference of hearing his dog 'howl in Irish' to the Welshwoman's singing: 'Without language, capable only of inarticulate and

---

[56] Said. *Orientalism*. 351.
[57] Ibid.
[58] Ibid.

unintelligible sounds, Sarah is scarcely distinguishable from the dumb beasts of the field, a point reinforced by the play's setting of an abandoned stable which now doubles as a classroom.'[59] Roche also comments on 'language as the key to memory, the means by which identity is not only formulated in the present but accumulates across time.'[60] Until Sarah can fully articulate her thoughts verbally, her identity remains stifled. But a more interesting stance on Sarah's inability to speak is offered by Seamus Heaney, who believes that Sarah represents Ireland: 'It is as if some symbolic figure of Ireland from an eighteenth-century vision poem, the one who confidently called herself Cathle'en ni Houlihan,[61] has been struck dumb by the shock of modernity.'[62] If we are to see Sarah as a Cathleen-figure, we must recognize the fact that, although Sarah makes progress throughout the course of the play, her 'language' is lost shortly after she discovers the 'union' of Maire and Yolland, representatives of Ireland and England.

One character who believes *her* identity is stifled in rural Ireland is Maire Chatach, an assertive young lady who has had a relationship with Manus but makes it clear that she wants other things—mainly, a life in America. When she first appears, Jimmy Jack greets her in Latin and she responds in the same language but adds, 'that's the height of my Latin. Fit me better if I had even that much English' (388). Although Maire speaks Gaelic, Latin, and Greek, she will not be satisfied until she has learned English. She ponders, 'The English soldiers below in the tents, them sapper fellas, they're coming up to give us a hand. I don't know a word they're saying, nor they me; but sure that doesn't matter, does it?' (389). Although these soldiers do not know Gaelic, they are the same individuals who will eradicate the Irish language to fulfill the colonial process. Maire's query[63] raises a connection between Mortimer's communication problem with his wife and foreshadows a later scene where Maire will attempt to cross her own linguistic barrier because she does not speak English. However, there is an intrinsic difference between Mortimer's and Maire's intentions in crossing linguistic boundaries. Shakespeare's Mortimer is a cultural anthropologist—he is not seeking assimilation in terms of identity. But for Friel's Maire, assimilation becomes a sign of emancipation rather than a desire.

The discussion raised about the new national school in the play that will certainly put the hedge schools out of operation makes the audience cognizant of the looming metamorphoses that will not elude Ireland for much longer. This will undoubtedly cause a change in the social dynamic of Baile Baeg; for as Bridget explains, 'And from the very first day you go, you'll not hear one word of Irish spoken. You'll be

59   Roche. 'A Bit Off the Map.' 142.
60   Ibid.
61   A mythical icon who represents the image of Ireland, Cathleen ni Houlihan has become the allegorical figure for Mother Ireland in Irish literature and folklore.
62   See Heaney's Review of *Translations*, by Brian Friel. *Times Literary Supplement*, 24 (1980): 1199.
63   Marie's challenge here reflects the underlying question of cultural awareness brought about by the 'What ish my nation?' inquiry made by Shakespeare's Macmorris in *Henry V*.

taught to speak English and every subject will be taught through English' (396). Like Maire, the students have been schooled in this rural setting on the classical Greek and Roman languages and literatures, in addition to exploring the richness of their own language and culture. Therefore, the prospect of this new form of education will be catastrophic to the development of their cultural awareness. McGrath states, 'In the new national schools Irish schoolchildren would learn the history of Ireland from texts written in English from the English point of view.'[64] This makes the impact of such an educational upheaval even more astounding, especially considering past texts like Edmund Spenser's *A View of the Present State of Ireland*—and numerous colonizing texts written from the same formula—which claims to provide insight into the island nation while, at the same time, undermines and stigmatizes every aspect of Irish life and society. McGrath also adds that 'Historians seem to agree that the national schools were more effective than any other means the British had used to eradicate Irish language and culture.'[65] Although several characters in *Translations* exhibit resistance to the idea of this educational system, some are open to the possibility—especially since they will have the opportunity to learn the English language. Yet for Friel, the cultural imposition of the educational system shapes the Gaelic identity of the students at the hedge school. More specifically, the closing of the schools in favor of England's National School signifies the loss of national/cultural identity for the Irish.

When Hugh, the often-intoxicated and verbose schoolmaster, first appears on the stage, he recounts his encounter with Captain Lancey, head of the Royal Engineers who are conducting the Ordnance Survey of County Donegal, and seems dumbfounded that this man 'does not speak Irish. Latin: I asked. None. Greek? Not a syllable. He speaks—on his own admission—only English' (399). Lancey parrots, to some degree, Harry Percy in *1 Henry IV*; for although both men speak English only, they fail to respect the Celtic Others who are bilingual, particularly because many of them do not speak their language. Hugh adds, 'English, I suggested, couldn't really express us' (399), which is one of the most ironic statements in the play. Despite his colonizing discourse, Lancey is not a real presence in *Translations*, unlike the xenophobic imperial agent Hotspur in *1 Henry IV*. By giving this line to Hugh, Friel is giving it an actor/audience/reader identification that is not there with Hotspur. In Shakespeare, the Other is sometimes untranslatable, as we see with Mortimer's Welsh wife. Friel adds a polemicizing depth to his play by letting the audience/ reader hear both sides of the issue.

Colin Meissner posits that Friel 'presents two assimilationists: Maire, a young woman who parrots Dan O'Connell[66] ... and Owen, whose ability to move flawlessly

---

64   McGrath. *Brian Friel's (Post)Colonial Drama*. 179–80.
65   Ibid.
66   Called 'The Liberator,' 'Daniel O'Connell, Gaelic folk hero and legendary lawyer, used the issue of emancipation to build a prototype popular mass movement, orchestrated by the Catholic Association (founded in 1823).'Colin Meissner. 'Wars Between Worlds: The Irish

between both cultures renders his actual identity questionable at best.'[67] Maire's yearning to be assimilated is seen once again, for she informs the class, 'We should all be learning to speak English. That's what my mother says. That's what I say. That's what Dan O'Connell said last month in Ennis. He said the sooner we all learn to speak English the better ... *The old language is a barrier to modern progress*[68] ... And he's right. I don't want Greek. I don't want Latin. I want English' (399). While Maire's assertiveness seems to be out of place in relation to her fellow classmates and neighbors, she represents that faction of the Irish populous, certainly instigated by O'Connell's moving rhetoric, who believed that their language and culture would prohibit them from advancing as a society and a nation. With bitter irony, the new language becomes, not merely a barrier, but an eradicator of cultural progress.

The second assimilationist, Owen, is a more complicated character, however. As an employer of the Royal Engineers surveying group, it is his job to assist Lieutenant Yolland in the mapmaking process that will 'standardize' the place-names of Ireland's geography. In other words, he will 'translate' the Gaelic names to English: 'My job is to translate the quaint, archaic tongue you people persist in speaking into the King's good English' (404). And translate he does, for when Lancey enters the schoolhouse, the following 'translation' occurs:

> *Lancey*: His Majesty's government has ordered the first ever comprehensive survey of this entire country—a general triangulation which will embrace detailed hydrographic and topographic information and which will be executed to a scale of six inches to the English mile.
> *Owen*: A new map is being made of the whole country.
> *Lancey*: This enormous task has been embarked on so that the military authorities will be equipped with up-to-date and accurate information on every corner of this part of the Empire.
> *Owen*: The job is being done by soldiers because they are skilled in this work.
> *Lancey*: And also so that the entire basis of land valuation can be reassessed for purposes of more equitable taxation.
> *Owen*: This new map will take the place of the estate agent's map so that from now on you will know exactly what is yours in law ...
> *Lancey*: 'Ireland is privileged. No such survey is being undertaken in England. So this survey cannot but be received as proof of the disposition of this government to advance the interests of Ireland.' My sentiments, too.
> *Owen*: This survey demonstrates the government's interest in Ireland and the captain thanks you for listening so attentively to him. (406–7)

I provide this 'translation' at length to demonstrate the hard fact of colonization that lies behind Lancey's seemingly benign jargon. This passage depicts how Lancey

---

Language, the English Army, and the Violence of Translation in Brian Friel's *Translations*.' *Colby Quarterly* 28 (1992): 157.

[67]   Meissner. 'Wars Between Worlds. 168–9.

[68]   Emphasis mine.

identifies Ireland in relation to the government's 'interests' in Ireland and its place in the Empire. The map becomes a topographical extension of the English ideological state apparatus and poses another treatment of England's imperial discourse. In direct contrast to the odious captain is Yolland, a meek soldier and displaced Englishman who has no interest in his position; in fact, he is anything but a colonial servant. He shyly offers, 'I can only say that I feel—I feel very foolish to— to— to— be working here and not speak your language. But I intend to rectify that—with Roland's help— indeed I do' (407). Yolland's empathy to Ireland is clear from the beginning of the play as a self-proclaimed Hibernophile, and although this suggests he is similar to Mortimer, the latter is intrigued only with the appeal of Welsh culture/music brought about by his wife. Mortimer does not wish to be assimilated.

While the residents of Baile Baeg are initially unaware of the deeper implications of the re-naming, Manus recognizes the danger and reacts at the end of Act I with a volatile temper:

Manus: What sort of a translation was that, Owen?
Owen: Did I make a mess of it?
Manus: You weren't saying what Lancey was saying!
Owen: 'Uncertainty in meaning is incipient poetry'—who said that?
Manus: There was nothing uncertain about what Lancey said: it's a bloody military operation, Owen! ... What's 'incorrect' about the place-names we have here?
Owen: Nothing at all. They're just going to be standardized.
Manus: You mean changed into English?
Owen: Where there's ambiguity, they'll be Anglicized. (408)

The 'ambiguity' Owen refers to certainly does not hold true for the residents of County Donegal, and as Said articulates, 'colonial space must be transformed sufficiently so as no longer to appear foreign to the imperial eye.'[69] But by anglicizing Ireland—to be clearer, to make Ireland England—the Ordnance Survey stands to make the colonial space foreign to the colonized.

At the end of Act I, the discussion which ensues between Owen and his brother Manus regarding Owen's 'translation' provides yet another clear example of the Empire's intentions, and Owen's inability to comprehend the results of this mapping project. As Manus points out, the English soldiers refer to Owen as 'Roland'— obviously through faulty translation; furthermore, they have not been corrected. At this early point in the play, Owen seems unaffected, and remarks, 'Owen—Roland— what the hell. It's only a name. It's the same me, isn't it? Well isn't it?' (408). Of course, in a play dominated by the implications of nominalism, a person's name is that individual's signifier, a sign of the past, present and future, and also a component of one's cultural identity. A similar process occurs with the naming of a nation. Owen's failure to realize what his name encapsulates and by extension what the naming of places represents for Ireland becomes his and their tragic flaw.

---

[69]   Said. *Culture and Imperialism.* 226.

The standardization of Irish place-names which strip away the cultural heritage of the Irish in Act II bears important connotations in terms of national identity. The official job descriptions for Yolland, a likable character, and Owen appear at the beginning of Act II, Scene 1: 'take each of the Gaelic names—every hill, stream, rock, even every patch of ground which possessed its own distinctive Irish name—and Anglicize it, either by changing it into its approximate English sound or by translating it into English words' (409). Through the 'changing' and 'translating' of the Gaelic place-names, dispossession of the territory's cultural reference/identification occurs. Owen provides an example of the process of anglicization: 'We are trying to denominate and at the same time describe that tiny area of soggy, rocky, sandy ground where that little stream enters the sea, an area known locally as Bun na hAbhann ... Burnfoot! What about Burnfoot?' (410). Unfortunately, Owen, who does not realize what the English are truly doing by modifying the map of Ireland until late in the play, fails to see how changing the name of an area alters and erodes its cultural legacy. But this mapping scene parallels III.i. of Shakespeare's *1 Henry IV*, and Yolland displays the same desire that Mortimer did to learn the language of the marginalized: 'Even if I did speak Irish I'd always be an outsider here, wouldn't I? I may learn the password but the language of the tribe will always elude me, won't it? The private core will always be ... hermetic, won't it?' (416). Yolland's preoccupation with the language and his problematic assimilation is reminiscent of Mortimer's frustration with his inability to speak his wife's native tongue. As McGrath asserts, 'Yolland articulates the cultural divide between Ireland and England when he realizes that ... he will never be assimilated.'[70] In fact, the Lieutenant's attraction to the Irish country and more specifically, to Maire, ends in tragedy.

In the case of Friel's play, the Irish place-names represent the 'foreign text' made readable for the 'target language' of the English. Consider the illustration that Hugh provides Lieutenant Yolland: 'But remember that words are signals, counters. They are not immortal. And it can happen ... that a civilization can be imprisoned in a linguistic contour which no longer matches the landscape of ... fact' (419). These remarks foreshadow the painful reality of what the translation work enlisted by the colonizers means for Ireland; for the 'Anglicized' place-names—Swinefort, Greencastle, White Plains, etc.—fail to hold the same meaning for the Gaelic occupants who live in these places. The Irish are, in a large sense, 'imprisoned,' and the new place-names do *not* match their landscape.

The loss of one's cultural heritage is further addressed by Yolland. Although he serves as an officer in the English army, Yolland finds the Irish countryside 'really heavenly' (414) and contrasts his own views with those of his father, who he describes as '[t]he perfect colonial servant' (415). Ironically, it is Yolland—rather than the native Irishman Owen—who recognizes that 'Something is being eroded' (420) in their push to standardize the Irish place-names. But as McGrath points out, 'Even within the Irish language the connection between the names and the significance of

---

[70]   McGrath. *Brian Friel's (Post)Colonial Drama*. 186.

places has begun to erode.'[71] Owen's tirade on the history of Tobair Vree expresses this issue:

> And we call that crossroads Tobair Vree. And why do we call it Tobair Vree? I'll tell you why. Tobair means a well. But what does Vree mean? It's a corruption of Brian—(*Gaelic pronunciation*)—Brian—at erosion of Tobair Bhriain. Because a hundred-and-fifty years ago there used to be a well there, not at the crossroads, mind you—that would be too simple—but in a field close to the crossroads. And an old man called Brian, whose face was disfigured by an enormous growth, got it into his head that the water in that well was blessed; and every day for seven months he went there and bathed his face in it. But the growth didn't go away; and one morning Brian was found drowned in that well. And ever since that crossroads is known as Tobair Vree—even though that well has long since dried up. I know the story because my grandfather told it to me. But ask Doalty—or Maire—or Bridget—even my father—even Manus—why it's called Tobair Vree; and do you think they'll know? I know they don't know. So the question I put to you, Lieutenant, is this: what do we do with a name like that? Do we scrap Tobair Vree altogether and call it—what?—The Cross? Crossroads? Or do we keep piety with a man long dead long forgotten, his name 'eroded' beyond recognition, whose trivial little story nobody in the parish remembers? (420)

This example represents the clearest illustration of the inherent outcome of the loss of cultural identity. The fact that 'Owen must produce the narrative of Brian in order to argue the irrelevance of the name, however, undoes his argument by revealing the role narrative plays as the 'scheme of identification' investing Tobair Vree with value—indeed, with historical value—for the community.'[72] Relative to the effects of linguistic erosion on a society, Benedict Anderson explains that because the re-naming of political/religious sites carried with them 'the meaning of "successor" to, or "inheritor of", something vanished. "New" and "old" are aligned diachronically, and the former appears always to invoke the ambiguous blessing from the dead.'[73] This diachronic alignment between old and new names breeds a cultural referent; therefore with Friel's play—and specifically Owen's explanation of the etymology of Tobair Vree—the cultural referent is in danger of being lost altogether.

There is also a relationship here with the French anxiety felt in *Henry V*. An examination of III.v discloses the deep-seeded fear of the colonizer as expressed through the discourse between the French King, the Dolphin, the Duke of Britain, and the Constable. Britain attests, 'if they march along/Unfought withal, but I will sell my dukedom,/To buy a slobb'ry and a dirty farm/In that nook-shotten isle of Albion' (III.v.11–14). At this point the French are dealing with their own issues of eviction; and while the Constable nonchalantly responds, 'Let us not hang like roping icicles/Upon our houses' thatch, whiles a more frosty people/Sweat drops of gallant

---

[71]   Ibid. 190.

[72]   Marc Silverstien. '"It's Only a Name": Schemes of Identification and the National Community in *Translations*.' *Essays in Theatre* 10 (1992): 137.

[73]   Anderson. *Imagined Communities*. 187.

youth in our rich fields!'(23–5), the others recognize the imminent danger. In fact, the Dolphin raises awareness of the possible threat of assimilation: 'Our madams mock at us, and plainly say/Our mettle is bred out, and they will give/Their bodies to the lust of English youth/To new-store France with bastard warriors' (28–31). The fear of bastardizing the French landscape and thus fulfilling the prophecy of assimilation is echoed by Britain, who states 'They bid us to the English dancing-schools,/And teach lavoltas high and swift corantos,/Saying our grace is only in our heels,/And that we are most lofty runaways' (32–5). As evidenced by Britain's concern, the French army's anxiety over English imperial domination is magnified by the fact that a deculturation will ensue as a result. In a sense, France will become a mirror image of England.

With regard to the colonial intentions cultural assumption, Meissner posits, 'The discourse of map-making presupposes ownership. In remapping Ireland, the Royal Engineers, acting on behalf of the British crown, make Ireland England and, in the authoritative position of the colonizer, offer the colonized a place to live.'[74] Therefore in *Translations*, as well as in *Henry V*, the colonizer re-shapes and re-imagines the nation under imperial rule. It becomes, to some extent, a distorted rebirth for the colonized nation. Consequently, the mapping scene in *Translations* culminates with a christening of sorts that raises deeper implications of the naming process:

> *Manus*: What's the celebration?
> *Owen*: A christening!
> *Yolland*: A baptism!
> *Owen*: A hundred christenings!
> *Yolland*: A thousand baptisms! Welcome to Eden!
> *Owen*: Eden's right! We name a thing and—bang!—it leaps into existence! (422)

But as Meissner assesses, 'The act of mapping and naming, the act of erasing the old and making the new, is equivalent to an ideologizing act of plunder: in other words, a redramatization of the colonial encounter.'[75] Meissner also asserts, 'In *Translations* the world is certainly a fallen one. For each new name, a former place leaps *out* of existence.'[76] The residents of Baile Baeg are caught between the Old and the New Ireland—a situation which will inevitably lead to chaos. As representatives of the political hegemony, both Owen and Yolland fail to recognize—at this point in the play—the long-term effects of their 'naming' and 're-naming.'

Closely mirroring III.i in *1 Henry IV*, along with some similarities in V.ii of *Henry V*, Maire and Yolland attempt to 'translate' their feelings for each other at the end of Act II. Consider the following snippet of the tender words between Maire, a young Irish girl who does not understand English, and Lieutenant Yolland, who does not understand Gaelic:

---

74   Meissner. 'Wars Between Worlds.' 170.
75   Ibid.
76   Ibid. 172.

Yolland: I wish to God you could understand me.

Maire: Soft hands; a gentleman's hands.

Yolland: Because if you could understand me I could tell you how I spend my days either thinking of you or gazing up at your house in the hope that you'll appear even for a second.

Maire: Every evening you walk by yourself along the Tra Bhan and every morning you wash yourself in front of your tent.

Yolland: I would tell you how beautiful you are, curly-headed Maire. I would so like to tell you how beautiful you are.

Maire: Your arms are long and thin and the skin on your shoulders is very white.

Yolland: I would tell you...

Maire: Don't stop—I know what you're saying. (429)

Linguistically, Maire and Yolland cannot understand each other because of the language barrier that exists between them. However, this passage illustrates the very core of translation. These two characters know what the other is saying, and although they do not know the word-for-word literal translation of this beautiful discourse, the very message is conveyed—and that's the important factor. According to Roche,

> The scene between [Maire and Yolland] climaxes in a kiss, as does that between Mortimer and his Welsh wife ... The latter's private scene is played out before an on-stage audience and reminds us that, however much genuine feeling Mortimer appears to display on the occasion, his marriage with Glendower's daughter was a political move to secure his release from captivity, convert enemies to allies and bolster the rebellion. The embrace between Yolland and Maire has an unintentional, uninvited audience of one; the political consequences of the private act Sarah witnesses follow later that same night and throughout the Act III of the following day. The primary difference is that Mortimer's marrying into the Welsh tribe has been sanctioned by both sides. In Friel's play, the opposite is the case.[77]

This final point of acceptance is elucidated through Jimmy Jack, who unwittingly asks Maire, 'Do you know the Greek word *endogamein*? It means to marry within the tribe. And the word *exogamein* means to marry outside the tribe. And you don't cross those borders casually—both sides get very angry' (446). Unfortunately, it is too late for Maire and Yolland; the borders are crossed and since assimilation is not a possibility, a metaphorical eviction occurs. Consequently, Yolland is 'evicted' from the culture he wishes to become a part of.

The final visible act of the colonizer—Lancey, in particular—in Friel's play lends an insightful shadow on the inevitable mark that political hegemony over foreign territories will leave. Silverstein discusses this chilling scene where Lancey threatens the oppressed Irish for information regarding Yolland's disappearance: 'This scene enacts the articulation of cultural difference at the moment of its annihilation, a difference registered most immediately at the level of the signifier' (136). What follows is a series of demands and threats that point to deterritorialization, eviction,

---

77   Roche. 'A Bit Off the Map.' 147.

and dispossession. Although the Donnelly twins[78]— who never actually appear on stage in the play—are undoubtedly to blame for Yolland's ill-fate, the Irish pupils at Hugh's school and the numerous families who will be affected by the imperialists' revenge have nothing to do with the situation. The scene begins with Lancey's stormy entrance at the school

> (Lancey indicates to Owen to translate. Owen hesitates, trying to assess the change in Lancey's manner and attitude.)
>
> *Lancey:* I'm in a hurry, O'Donnell.
>
> *Owen*: The captain has an announcement to make.
>
> *Lancey*: Lieutenant Yolland is missing. We are searching for him. If we don't find him, or if we receive no information as where he is to be found, I will pursue the following course of action. *(He indicates to Owen to translate.)*
>
> *Owen*: They are searching for George. If they don' find him—
>
> *Lancey*: Commencing twenty-four hours from now we will shoot all livestock in Ballybeg.
>
> (Owen stares at Lancey.)
>
> *Owen*: Beginning this time tomorrow they'll kill every animal in Baile Baeg—unless they're told where George is.
>
> *Lancey*: If that doesn't bear results, commencing forty-eight hours from now we will embark on a series of evictions and leveling of every abode in the following selected areas—
>
> *Owen*: You're not—!
>
> *Lancey*: Do your job. Translate.
>
> *Owen*: If they still haven't found him in two days time they'll begin evicting and leveling every house starting with these townlands.
>
> (Lancey reads from his list.)
>
> *Lancey*: Swinefort.
>
> *Owen*: Lis na Muc.
>
> *Lancey*: Burnfoot.
>
> *Owen*: Bun na hAbhann.
>
> *Lancey*: Dromduff.
>
> *Owen* Druim Dubh.
>
> *Lancey*: Whiteplains.
>
> *Owen*: Machaire Ban.
>
> *Lancey*: Kings Head.
>
> *Owen*: Cnoc na Ri. (439)

Owen, the former colonial servant, now achieves the full realization that he is an Irishman. As Meissner states, 'Owen's attempted assimilation ends in his exclusion from both worlds ... Friel seems to be suggesting , that the borders are drawn; one

---

[78]   It is my assumption that the Donnelly twins remain a silent entity throughout *Translations* as a means of articulating the fact that, regardless of how many Irish people naively believed that the English presence in their nation would yield 'modern progress,' a strong sense of resistance was felt from the onset of the imperial thrust in Ireland.

is either one or the other, as Owen's experience ultimately demonstrates, and as the violent culmination of the budding love between Yolland and Maire makes real' (169). Owen's personal history/identity is in direct conflict with colonial ideology. Just as the language of the colonizer becomes more harmful and diabolical with each play in Shakespeare's *Henriad*, culminating with *Henry V*, Lancey's message conjures the same harshness and hints of domination. In particular, this scene eerily echoes King Henry's menacing speech at Harfleur, where he vows, 'If I begin the battr'y once again,/I will not leave the half-achieved Harflew/Till in her ashes she lies buried' (III.iii.7–9) and concludes, 'What say you? Will you yield, and this avoid?/Or guilty in defense, be thus destroy'd?' (III.iii.42–3). Henry's comment on imperialism appears as serious and barbaric as Lancey's; both leaders will not allow leniency if their orders are not followed.

Where Shakespeare's history plays culminate with a pervasive sense of triumph, Friel's *Translations* leaves the questions raised throughout the piece unanswered. This may be due largely to the sense that, to this present day, the Irish question still waits to find an answer, just as the ideal of an Irish national identity remains fragmented and hybridized. The ideology of the Irish people, reflected vividly in the publication of an increasing number of literary texts over the past century, strives to find cohesion. Perhaps Hugh clarifies the Irish plight best in *Translations*: 'it is not the literal past, the "facts" of history, that shape us, but images of the past embodied in language ... we must never cease renewing those images; because once we do, we fossilize' (445); therefore, with the reformulation of the past and constant redressing of these cultural issues, a collective Irish identity may be achieved.

Conclusion

mingling the immigrant
guttural with the vowels
of homesickness who neither
knows nor cares that

a new language
is a kind of scar
and heals after a while
into a passable imitation
of what went before.[1]

In *Culture and Imperialism*, Edward Said asserts, 'To achieve recognition is to rechart and then occupy the place in imperial cultural forms reserved for subordination, to occupy it self-consciously, fighting for it on the very same territory once ruled by a consciousness that assumed the subordination of a designated inferior Other. Hence, reinscription.'[2] The literary and artistic enterprises coming out of Ireland in the twentieth century reflect Said's ideas as it desires this recognition as an enabling factor for overcoming the nation's marginalized position. In particular, the manifestation of this reterritorialization can be seen through the overt reinscription of William Shakespeare's plays by Irish dramatists who engage the issues of reconstituting national identity that is separate from that imposed on them through imperial domination.

As this study illustrates, Shakespeare's plays embody an empathy for the Irish Other. While this sentiment is most blatant in the *Henriad*, Shakespeare serves as an antithesis to Edmund Spenser in particular by problematizing—and debunking—the tenets of deterritorialization and colonial oppression which he sets forth in *A View of the Present State of Ireland*. This is not an anomaly, for twentieth-century Irish dramatists astutely recognize that Shakespeare has provided a voice for the Other. Therefore, with his commiseration for marginalized peoples and the anti-colonial underpinnings in his texts, Shakespeare falls between the English discourse which claims him and the Irish discourse which assimilates him.

Even though Shakespeare, based on my reading, can be seen as a colonial dissenter by questioning the modes of imperialist discourse about the British Isles, the effects that this has on an Irish culture trying to distinguish itself from under the imperialist grasp needs to be addressed as I conclude. In one sense, this fact is

---

[1]   From Eavan Boland's 'Mise Eire' in *Outside History: Selected Poems 1980–1990*. New York: Norton, 1990. 78.

[2]   Said. *Culture and Imperialism*. 210.

limiting for Ireland; for throughout the twentieth century, Irish writers are still using an Englishman to define their Irishness. However, what the Irish gain essentially is a recognition that to be Irish is to be forever linked to England's colonial history—a turbulent history which has shaped Modern Ireland nonetheless.

Twentieth-century Irish plays contain symbolic representations for the present state of Ireland, as articulated through O'Casey's Mary and Friel's Sarah. This is a good example of how Ireland has not quite grown accustomed to her relation to England and how perhaps this uneasy relationship has now expanded to include Northern Ireland, who is now trying to get a piece of the identity action, so to speak. This occurs through Field Day, which positions itself to push for a kind of independence outside of the historical antagonism that is distinctly an Anglo-Irish issue.

I speculate that there will be some form of Irish identity separate from and outside of England, and that Irish authors will be able to write their own literature without relying on English writers. Just as Mary Boyle (Mother Ireland) and the child in Sean O'Casey's *Juno and the Paycock* represent an independent identity that can thrive without Father England, perhaps the efforts of those Irish citizens (like those who have instituted the Field Day Theatre Company) intent on establishing an emergent national identity will succeed in marking a clear delineation between what is English and what is Irish. And while Sarah cannot speak at the beginning of Friel's *Translations*, her fellow Irishman teaches her how to articulate *her* language— Gaelic—and thus, express a voice outside of an English model.

Further Reading

Ahmad, Aijaz. *In Theory: Classes, Nations, Literatures.* London: Verso, 1992.
——. 'The Politics of Literary Postcoloniality.' *Race and Class* 36.3 (1995): 1–20.
Andrews, J.H. *Irish Maps.* Dublin: Eason and Son, 1978.
Ashcroft, Bill, Gareth Griffiths, and Helen Tiffin. *The Empire Writes Back: Theory and Practice in Post-Colonial Literatures.* London: Routledge, 1989.
Avery, Bruce. 'Mapping the Irish Other: Spenser's *A View of the Present State of Ireland.*' *English Literary History* 57.2 (1990): 263–79.
Bacon, Francis. *A Briefe Discourse, Touching the Happie Union of the Kingdomes of England and Scotland. Dedicated in Private to His Majestie.* London, 1603.
Baker, Alan R.H. and Gideon Biger. *Ideology and Landscape in Historical Perspective: Essays on the Meanings of Some Places in the Past.* Cambridge: Cambridge UP, 1992.
Baker, David J. 'Off the Map: Charting Uncertainty in Renaissance Ireland.' *Representing Ireland: Literature and the Origins of Conflict, 1534–1660.* Ed. Brendan Bradshaw, Andrew Hadfield, and Willy Maley. Cambridge: Cambridge UP, 1993. 76–92.
——. '"Wildehirisheman": Colonialist Representation in Shakespeare's *Henry V.*' *English Literary Renaissance* 22 (1992): 37–61.
Bakhtin, Mikhail. *Rabelais and His World.* Trans. Helene Iswolsky. Bloomington: Indiana UP, 1942.
Barber, Peter. 'England II: Monarchs, Ministers, and Maps, 155–1625.' *Monarchs, Ministers, and Maps: The Emergence of Cartography as a Tool of Government in Early Modern Europe.* Ed. David Buisseret. Chicago: University of Chicago Press, 1992.
Barnard, T.C. 'The Hartlib Circle and the Cult and Culture of Improvement in Ireland.' *Samuel Hartlib and the Universal Reformation.* Ed. Mark Greengrass, Michael Leslie, and Timothy Raylor. Cambridge: Cambridge UP, 1994.
Bartlett, Thomas. *The Fall and Rise of The Irish Nation: The Catholic Question, 1690–1830.* Dublin: Gill and Macmillan, 1992.
Bartley, J.O. *Teague, Shenkin and Sawney: Being an Historical Study of the Earliest Irish, Welsh and Scottish Characters in English Plays.* Cork: Cork UP, 1954.
Beare, Philip O'Sullivan. *Historiae Catholicae Iberniae Compendium.* 1621. Trans. M.J. Byrne as *Ireland Under Elizabeth.* Dublin: Sealy, Bryers & Co., 1903; reissued, Port Washington, NY and London: Kennikat Press, 1970.
——. *Selections from the Zoilomastix of Philip O'Sullivan Beare.* Ed. Thomas J. O'Donnell. Dublin: Irish Manuscripts Commission, 1960.
Belsey, Catherine. *The Subject of Tragedy: Identity and Difference in Renaissance Drama.* London: Methuen, 1995.

Berry, Edward I. *Patterns of Decay: Shakespeare's Early Histories*. Charlottesville: UP of Virginia, 1975.

Bhabha, Homi K. *Nation and Narration*. London: Routledge, 1990.

Boyce, D. George and Allan O'Day. *The Making of Modern Irish History: Revisionism and Revisionist Controversy*. London: Routledge, 1992.

Bradshaw, Brendan. 'The Elizabethans and the Irish.' *Studies* 66 (1977): 38–50.

———. 'The Elizabethans and the Irish: A Muddled Model.' *Studies* 70 (1981): 233–44.

Bradshaw, Brendan, and John Morrill, eds. 'The Tudor Reformation and Revolution in Wales and Ireland: The Origins of the British Problem.' *The British Problem, c. 1534–1707: State Formation in the Atlantic Archipelago*. London: Macmillan, 1996. 39–65.

Bradshaw, Brendan, and Peter Roberts, eds. *British Consciousness and Identity: The Making of Britain, 1533–1707*. Cambridge: Cambridge UP, 1998.

———. 'The English Reformation and Identity Formation in Ireland and Wales.' *British Consciousness and Identity. The Present State of England, Parts III & IV*. London, 1683.

Bradshaw, Brendan, Andrew Hadfield, and Willy Maley, eds. *Representing Ireland: Literature and the Origins of Conflict, 1534–1600*. Cambridge: Cambridge UP, 1993.

Brady, Ciarán, and Raymond Gillespie, eds. 'Court, Castle and Country.' *Natives and Newcomers: Essays on the Making of Irish Colonial Society, 1534–1641*. Dublin: Irish Academy Press, 1986. 22–49.

———. *Natives and Newcomers: Essays on the Making of Irish Colonial Society 1534–1641*. Dublin: Irish Academic Press, 1986.

Brink, Jean R. 'Constructing the *View of the Present State of Ireland*.' *Spenser Studies* 11 (1990): 203–28.

Bristoll, John [John Thornborough, Bishop of Bristol]. *The Ioiefull and Blessed Reunited of Two Mighty & Famous Kingdomes, England & Scotland into their Ancient Name of Great Brittaine*. Oxford: n.d.

Brown, M. *The Politics of Irish Literature*. Seattle: University of Washington Press, 1972.

Brown, Paul. 'This Thing of Darkness I Acknowledge Mine: *The Tempest* and the Discourse of Colonialism.' *Political Shakespeare: Essays on Cultural Materialism*. Ed. Jonathan Dollimore and Alan Sinfield. Manchester: Manchester UP, 1985. 48–71.

Brown, Terence. *Ireland: A Social and Cultural History 1922–1985*. London: Fontana, 1981.

Burnett, Mark Thornton, and Ramona Wray, eds. *Shakespeare and Ireland: History, Politics, Culture*. Basingstoke: Macmillan, 1997.

Butler, Richard, ed. *Tracts Relating to Ireland*. Dublin: Irish Archaeological Society, 1843.

Calderwood, James. *Metadrama in Shakespeare's Henriad*. Berkeley: University of California Press, 1979.

Canny, Nicholas. 'Edmund Spenser and the Development of an Anglo-Irish Identity.' *Yearbook of English Studies* 13 (1983): 1–19.

Canny, Nicholas, and Anthony Pagden, eds. *Colonial Identity in the Atlantic World, 1550–1800*. Princeton, NJ: Princeton UP, 1987.

———. '"Such was Irena's Countenance": Ireland in Spenser's Prose and Poetry.' *Texas Studies in Literature and Language* 28.1 (1986): 24–50.

Carrol, Paul Vincent. 'Can the Abbey Theater be Restored?' *The Abbey Theater: Interviews and Recollections*. Ed. E.H. Mikahil. Totowa, NJ: Barnes and Noble, 1988. 188–92.

Casey, D., and R. Rhodes, eds. *Views of the Irish Peasantry 1800–1916*. Hamden, CT.: Archon, 1977.

Chatterjee, Partha. *The Nation and its Fragment: Colonial and Postcolonial Histories*. Princeton: Princeton UP, 1993.

Colley, Linda. 'Britishness and Otherness: An Argument.' *Journal of British Studies* 31 (1992): 309–29.

Coughlan, Patricia. *Spenser and Ireland: An Interdisciplinary Perspective*. Cork: Cork UP, 1989.

Coulter, C. 'Class, Ethnicity and Political Identity in Northern Ireland.' *Irish Journal of Sociology* 4 (1994): 1–26.

Crozier, M., ed. *Cultural Traditions in Northern Ireland*. Belfast: Institute of Irish Studies, 1989.

Cullen, L.M. *The Emergence of Modern Ireland, 1600–1900*. London: Bastford, 1981.

Cullen, Patrick. 'The Political War Ballads of Sean O'Casey, 1916–18.' *Irish University Review* (1983): 168–79.

Cullingford, E.B. '"Thinking of her as Ireland": Yeats, Pearse and Heany.' *Textual Practice* 4.1 (1987): 443–60.

Cummins, P., B. Jones, P. Murphy, and A. Smyth. 'Image Making, Image Breaking.' *Circa* 32 (1987): 13–19.

Davies, Sir John. *A Discovery of the True Causes Why Ireland Was Never Entirely Subdued [And] Bought Under Obedience of the Crown of England Until the Beginning of His Majesty's Happy Reign*. 1612. Ed. James P. Meyers Jr. Reprint, Washington, DC: Catholic University of America Press, 1988.

Dollimore, Jonathan, and Alan Sinfield. 'History and Ideology: The Instance of *Henry V.*' *Alternative Shakespeares*. Ed John Drakakis. London: Routledge, 1985. 206–27.

———, eds. *Political Shakespeare: [New] Essays in Cultural Materialism*. Manchester: Manchester UP, 1985; 2nd ed.: 1995.

Duncan, James and Ley, David, eds. *Place/Culture/Representation*. London: Routledge, 1993.

Ellis, Steven. '"Not Mere English": The British Perspective 1400–1650.' *History Today* 38 (1988): 41–8.

Ellis, Steven G., and Sarah Barber, eds. *Conquest & Union: Fashioning a British State, 1485–1725*. London: Longman, 1995.

Emitie, Thomas. *A New Remonstrance from Ireland*. London, 1642.

English, Richard. 'Shakespeare and the Definition of the Irish Nation.' *Shakespeare and Ireland: History, Politics, Culture*. Ed. Mark Thornton Burnett and Ramona Wray. New York: St Martin's, 1997. 136–51.

FitzGerald, Mary. 'Sean O'Casey and Lady Gregory: The Record of Friendship.' *Sean O'Casey: Centenary Essays*. Ed. David Krause and Robert G. Lowery. Gerrards Cross: Colin Smythe, 1980. 121–64.

Fogarty, Ann. 'The Colonization of Language: Narrative Strategies in *A View of the Present State of Ireland* and the *The Faerie Queene*, Book VI.' *Spenser and Ireland: An Interdisciplinary Perspective*. Ed. Patricia Coughlan. Cork: Cork UP, 1989. 75–109.

Foucault, Michel. *The Order of Things: An Archaeology of the Human Sciences*. New York: Vintage, 1970.

Frame, Robin. *Colonial Ireland, 1169–1369*. Dublin: Helicon, 1981.

Frazier, Adrian. *Behind the Scenes: Yeats, Horniman, and the Struggle for the Abbey Theater*. Berkeley: University of California Press, 1990.

Gallagher, M. 'How many nations are there in Ireland?' *Ethnic and Racial Studies* 18.4 (1995): 715–39.

Geertz, Clifford. *The Interpretation of Cultures*. New York: Basic Books, 1973.

Gellner, Ernest. *Nations and Nationalism*. Ithaca: Cornell UP, 1983.

Gerstenberger, Donna. 'W.B. Yeats: Politics and History.' *Irish Writers and Politics*. Ed. Okimufi Komesu and Masaru Sekine. Savages, MD: Barnes and Noble, 1990. 80–93.

Gibbons, Luke. *Transformations in Irish Culture*. Cork: Cork UP/Field Day, 1996.

Gottfried, Rudolph B. 'The Early Development of the Section on Ireland in Camden's *Britannia*.' *English Literary History* 10 (1943): 17–30.

Gramsci, Antonio. *Selections from the Prison Notebook of Antonio Gramsci*. Trans. Quintin Hoare and Geoffrey Nowell Smith. New York: International Publishers, 1971.

Grant, Alexander, and Keith J. Stringer, eds. *Uniting the Kingdom? The Making of British History*. London: Routledge, 1995.

——. *Renaissance Self-Fashioning: From More to Shakespeare*. Chicago: University of Chicago Press, 1980.

Gruffydd, R. Geraint. 'The Renaissance and Welsh Literature.' *The Celts and the Renaissance: Tradition and Innovation*. Ed. Glanmor Williams and Robert Owen Jones. Cardiff: University of Wales Press, 1990.

G.S. *A Briefe Declaration of the Barbarous and Inhumane Dealings of the Northerne Irish Rebels*. London, 1641.

Guibernau, M. *Nationalisms: The Nation State and Nationalism in the Twentieth Century*. Oxford: Polity, 1996.

Hadfield, Andrew. 'English Colonialism and National Identity in Early Modern Ireland.' *Éire-Ireland* 28.1 (1993): 69–86.

———. *Literature, Politics and National Identity: Reformation to Renaissance*. Cambridge: Cambridge UP, 1994.

———. 'Spenser, Ireland, and Sixteenth-Century Political Theory.' *Modern Language Review* 89.1 (1994): 1–18.

———. 'Spenser's *View of the Present State of Ireland*: Some Notes Toward a Materialistic Analysis of Discourse.' *Anglo-Irish and Irish Literature: Aspects of Language and Culture*. Vol. 2. Ed. Brigit Bramsback and Martin Croghan. Uppsala: Uppsala UP, 1988. 265–72.

———. 'Translating the Reformation: John Bale's Irish *Vocacyon*.' *Representing Ireland: Literature and the Origins of Conflict, 1534–1660*. Ed. Brendan Bradshaw, Andrew Hadfield, and Willy Maley.. Cambridge: Cambridge UP, 1993. 43–59.

Hadfield, Andrew, and John McVeagh, eds. *'Strangers to That Land': British Perception of Ireland from the Reformation to the Famine*. Gerrard's Cross: Colin Smythe, 1994.

———. *A Short View of the State of Ireland*. London, 1605.

Heaney, Seamus. Review of *Translations* by Brian Friel. *Times Literary Supplement* 24 (1980): 1199.

Highley, Christopher. *Shakespeare, Spenser & the Crisis in Ireland*. Cambridge: Cambridge UP, 1997.

Hogan, Robert. *'Since O'Casey' and Other Essays on Irish Drama*. Totowa, NJ: Barnes and Noble, 1983.

Holderness, Graham. 'What ish my nation?: Shakespeare and National Identities.' *Textual Practice* 5.1 (1991): 74–99.

Hutchinson, J. *The Dynamics of Cultural Nationalism: The Gaelic Revival and the Creation of the Irish National State*. London: Allen and Unwin, 1987.

James, Mervyn. *Society, Politics and Culture: Studies in Early Modern England*. Cambridge: Cambridge UP, 1986.

Jardine, Lisa. 'Encountering Ireland: Gabriel Harvey, Edmund Spenser and English Colonial Ventures.' *Representing Ireland: Literature and the Origins of Conflict, 1534–1660*. Ed. Brendan Bradshaw, Andrew Hadfield, and Willy Maley. Cambridge: Cambridge UP, 1993. 60–75.

Johnston, R.J., D.B. Knight, and E. Kofman, eds. *Nationalism, Self-Determination and Political Geography*. London: Croom Helm, 1988.

Jones, Ann Rosalind, and Peter Stallybrass. 'Dismantling Irena: The Sexualizing of Ireland in Early Modern England.' *Nationalisms and Sexualities*. Ed. Andrew Parker, Mary Russo, Doris Sommer, and Patricia Yaeger. London: Routledge, 1992. 157–171.

Jonson, Ben. 'To the Memory of My Beloved the Author, Mr. William Shakespeare, and What He Hath Left Us.' *Seventeenth Century Prose and Poetry*. Ed. Alexander

M. Witherspoon and Frank J. Warnke. San Diego: Harcourt Brace Jovanvich, 1982. 768–9.

Kastan, David Scott. *Shakespeare After Theory*. London: Routledge, 1999.

———. *Shakespeare and the Shapes of Time*. Hanover, NH: UP of New England, 1982.

Klein, Bernhard. 'English Cartographers and the Mapping of Ireland in the Early Modern Period.' *Journal for the Study of British Cultures* 2.2 (1995): 115–39.

Kurland, Stuart M. '*Hamlet* and the Scottish Succession?' *Studies in English Literature* 34 (1994): 279–300.

Leerssen, Joeseph T. *Mere Irish and Fíor-Ghael: Studies in the Idea of Irish Nationality, its Development and Literary Expression prior to the Nineteenth Century.* Amsterdam: John Benjamins, 1986.

Leonard, M. *Mother Ireland*. Coventry: Coventry Museums and Galleries, 1994.

Longley, Edna, ed. *Culture in Ireland: Division or Diversity?* Belfast: Institute of Irish Studies, 1991.

Loomba, Ania. *Race, Gender, Renaissance Drama*. Manchester: Manchester UP, 1989.

Lupton, Julia Reinhard. 'Mapping Mutability: Or, Spenser's Irish Plot.' *Representing Ireland: Literature and the Origins of Conflict, 1534–1660*. Ed. Brendan Bradshaw, Andrew Hadfield, and Willy Maley. Cambridge: Cambridge UP, 1993. 93–115.

McLeod, Bruce. *The Geography of Empire in English Literature, 1580–1745*. Cambridge: Cambridge UP, 1999.

Maley, Willy. 'Shakespeare, Holinshed and Ireland: Resource and Contexts.' *Shakespeare and Ireland: History, Politics and Culture*. Ed. Mark Thornton Burnett and Ramona Wray. Basingstoke: Macmillan, 1997. 27–46.

———. 'Spenser and Ireland: A Selected Bibliography.' *Spenser Studies* 9 (1991): 227–42.

———. 'Spenser and Ireland: An Annotated Bibliography, 1986–96.' *Irish University Review* 26.2 (1996): 342–53.

——— '"This sceptred isle": Shakespeare and the British Problem.' *Shakespeare and National Culture*. Ed. John J. Joughin. Manchester: Manchester UP, 1997. 83–108.

Marcus, Leah S., Janel Mueller, and Mary Beth Rose, eds. *Elizabeth I: Collected Works*. Chicago: University of Chicago Press, 2000.

Marsden, Jean I., ed. *The Appropriation of Shakespeare: Post-Renaissance Reconstructions of the Works and the Myth*. Hemel Hempstead: Harvester Wheatsheaf, 1991.

Mead, P. and M. Campbell. *Shakespeare's Books: Contemporary Cultural Politics and the Persistence of Empire*. Melbourne: Melbourne UP, 1993.

Murphy, Andrew. 'Shakespeare's Irish History.' *Literature and History* 5.1 (1996): 38–59.

——. '"Tish Ill Done": *Henry the Fift* and the Politics of Editing.' *Shakespeare and Ireland: History, Politics, Culture.* Ed. Mark Thornton Burnett and Romana Wray. Basingstoke: Macmillan, 1997. 213–34.

Myers, James P., ed. *Elizabethan Ireland: A Selection of Elizabethan Writers on Ireland.* Hamden, CT: Archon, 1983.

Neeson, Eoin. *The Civil War in Ireland 1922–1923.* Cork: Mercier Press, 1966.

O'Casey, Sean. *I Knock at the Door. Autobiographies.* Vol. 1. New York: Carroll & Graf, 1984. 3–178.

Parker, A., M. Russo, D. Sommer, and P. Yaegar. *Nationalisms and Sexualities.* London: Routledge, 1992.

Parker, Patricia. *Shakespeare from the Margins: Language, Culture, Context.* Chicago: University of Chicago Press, 1996.

Patterson, Annabel. 'Back by Popular Demand: The Two Versions of *Henry V.*' *Shakespeare and the Popular Voice.* Oxford: Basil Blackwell, 1989.

Pittock, Murray G.H. *Celtic Identity and the British Image.* Manchester: Manchester UP, 1999.

Queen Elizabeth's Proclamations 1559–1602. 1603.

Said, Edward. *The World, the Text, and the Critic.* Cambridge, MA: Harvard UP, 1983.

Scheper-Hughes, Nancy. *Saints, Scholars, and Schizophrenia: Mental Illness in Rural Ireland.* Berkeley: University of California Press, 1979.

Sharkey, S. *Ireland and Iconography of Rape: Colonisation, Constraint and Gender.* London: University of North London Press, 1994.

Sibley, D. *Geographies of Exclusion.* London: Routledge, 1995.

Sidney, Henry. *Memoire.* London, 1583; reprinted London, 1855.

Sinfield, Alan. *Faultlines: Cultural Materialism and the Politics of Dissident Reading.* Berkeley: University of California Press, 1992.

Smythe, W.J., and K. Whelan, eds. *Common Ground: Essays on the Historical Geography of Ireland.* Cork: Cork UP, 1988.

Speed, John. *Theatre of the Empire of Great Britaine.* London, 1611.

——. *The Faerie Queene.* Ed. Thomas P. Roche and C. Patrick O'Donnell. New Haven, CT: Yale UP, 1978.

Stephans, N. and Robin E. Glasscock, eds. *Irish Geographical Studies.* Belfast: Queen's University, 1970.

Strong, Roy. *The Renaissance Garden in England.* London: Thames and Hudson, 1979.

Taylor, Gary. *Reinventing Shakespeare: A Cultural History from the Restoration to the Present.* New York, Weidenfeld and Nicolson, 1989; Oxford, Oxford UP, 1991.

Temple, Sir John. *The Irish Rebellion.* London, 1646.

Thiong'o, Ngugi wa. *Decolonising the Mind.* London: James Currey, 1987.

Trotter, Mary. '"Double Crossing" Irish Borders: The Field Day Production of Tom Kilroy's *Double Cross.*' *New Hibernia Review* 1.1 (1997): 31–43.

Tuan, Yi-Fi. 'Language and the Making of Place: A Narrative-Descriptive Approach." *Annals of the Association of American Geographers* 81 (1991): 684–96.

Valiulis, M.G. 'Power, Gender and Identity in the Irish Free State'. *Journal of Women's History* 6.41/7.1 (1995): 117–36.

Wernham, R.B. *The Making of Elizabethan Foreign Policy 1558–1603*. Los Angeles: Berkeley and University of California Press, 1980.

Whelan, K. 'The Power of Place.' *Irish Review* 12 (1992): 13–20.

Williams, Raymond. *Marxism and Literature*. Oxford: Oxford UP, 1977.

Bibliography

Agas, Ralph. *A Preparative to Plotting of Landes and Tenements for surveigh, shewing the Diversitie of sundrie instruments supplied thereunto.* London, 1596.

An Answer to the Memoirs of Mrs. Billington. London, 1792.

Anderson, Benedict. *Imagined Communities: Reflections on the Origin and Spread of Nationalism.* London: Verso, 1991.

Andrews, J.H. *Shapes of Ireland: Maps and Their Makers 1564–1839.* Dublin: Geography Publications, 1997.

Ayling, Ronald. 'Sean O'Casey and the Abbey Theatre, Dublin.' *Sean O'Casey: Centenary Essays.* Ed. David Krause and Robert G. Lowery. Gerrards Cross: Colin Smythe, 1980. 13–40.

——. 'Sean O'Casey's Dublin Trilogy.' *Sean O'Casey: A Collection of Critical Essays.* Ed. Thomas Kilroy. Englewood Cliffs, NJ: Prentice-Hall, 1975. 77–89.

Bale, John. *Vocacyon.* London, 1553.

Barton, Sir D. Plunket. *Links Between Ireland and Shakespeare.* Dublin: Maunsel & Co., 1919.

Beight, Curtis. 'Elizabethan World Pictures.' *Shakespeare and National Culture.* Ed. John J. Joughin. Manchester: Manchester UP, 1997. 295–325.

Bernstein, Mashey. '"What a Parrot Talks": The Janus Nature of Anglo-Irish Writing.' *The Text and Beyond: Essays in Literary Linguistics.* Ed. Cynthia Golden Bernstein. Tuscaloosa: University of Alabama Press, 1994. 263–77.

Bhabha, Homi. *The Location of Culture.* London: Routledge, 1994.

Binnie, Eric. 'Brecht and Friel: Some Irish Parallels.' *Modern Drama* 31 (1988): 365–70.

Blitch, Alice Fox. 'O'Casey's Shakespeare.' *Modern Drama* 15 (1972): 283–90.

Boland, Eavan. 'Mise Eire.' *Outside History: Selected Poems 1980–1990.* New York: Norton, 1990. 78.

Cairns, David and Shaun Richards. *Writing Ireland: Colonialism, Nationalism, and Culture.* Manchester: Manchester UP, 1988.

Cambrensis, Giraldus. *Expugnatio Hiberniae.* c. 1189.

——. *Topographia Hiberniae.* c. 1187.

Campion, Edmund. *A History of Ireland.* London, 1571.

Canny, Nicholas. 'Irish, Scottish and Welsh Responses to Centralisation, *c.* 1530–*c*.1640: A Comparative Perspective.' *Uniting the Kingdom? The Making of British History.* Ed. Alexander Grant and Keith J. Stringer. London & New York: Routledge, 1995. 147–69.

Cavanagh, Shelia T. '"The Fatal Destiny of that Land": Elizabethan Views of Ireland.' *Representing Ireland: Literature and the Origins of Conflict, 1534–1660.* Ed.

Brendan Bradshaw, Andrew Hadfield, and Willy Maley. Cambridge: Cambridge UP, 1993. 116–31.

Clarke, Brenna Katz. *The Emergence of the Irish Peasant Play at the Abbey Theatre.* Ann Arbor: UMI Research Press, 1982.

Connolly, S.J. 'Culture, Identity and Tradition: Changing Definitions of Irishness.' *In Search of Ireland: A Cultural Geography.* Ed. Brian Graham. London: Routledge, 1997. 43–63.

Cronin, Michael. 'Rug-headed kerns speaking tongues: Shakespeare, Translation and the Irish Language.' *Shakespeare and Ireland: History, Politics, Culture.* Ed. Mark Thornton Burnett and Ramona Wray. New York: St Martin's, 1997. 193–212.

Curran, Frank. *Derry: Countdown to Disaster.* Dublin: Gill, 1986.

Deane, Seamus. 'Heroic Styles: The Tradition of an Idea.' *Ireland's Field Day.* London: Field Day Theatre Company, 1985. 45–58.

——. 'Introduction.' *Nationalism, Colonialism, and Literature.* Ed. Terry Eagleton, Frederic Jameson, and Edward W. Said. Introduction Seamus Deane. Minneapolis: University of Minnesota Press, 1990. 3–19.

Derricke, John. *The Image of Ireland.* London: 1581; reprinted Edinburgh: Adam and Charles Black, 1883.

Dowling, P. J. *The Hedge Schools of Ireland.* Cork: Mercier Press, 1968.

Edwards, Philip. *Threshold of a Nation.* Cambridge: Cambridge UP, 1979.

Fallon, Brian. *An Age of Innocence: Irish Culture 1930–1960.* New York: St Martin's, 1998.

Fanon, Frantz. *Black Skin, White Masks.* New York: Grove Press, 1967.

——. 'On National Culture.' *The Post-Colonial Studies Reader.* Ed. Bill Ashcroft, Gareth Griffiths, and Helen Tiffin. London: Routledge, 1995. 153–6.

Fay, Gerard. *The Abbey Theatre: Cradle of Genius.* Dublin: Clonmore and Reynolds, 1958.

Field Day Anthology of Irish Writing. Ed. Seamus Deane. New York: W.W. Norton & Company, 1992.

Field Day Anthology of Irish Writing: Irish Women's Writing and Traditions. Vols 4 & 5. Ed. Angela Bourke, Siobhan Kilfeather, Maria Luddy, et al. Cork: Cork UP, 2002.

Fitzgibbon, Emelie. 'Theatre with its Sleeves Rolled Up.' *Irish Writers and Politics.* Ed. Okifumi Komesu and Masaru Sekine. Savage, MD: Barnes and Noble, 1990. 306–15.

Forster, R.F. *The Oxford History of Ireland.* Oxford: Oxford UP, 1989.

Friel, Brian. *Translations. Selected Plays.* London: Faber and Faber, 1984. 377–447.

Gellner, Ernest. *Thought and Change.* London: Weidenfeld and Nicholson, 1964.

Greenblatt, Stephen. 'Invisible Bullets: Renaissance Authority and its Subversion, *Henry IV* and *Henry V*.' *Political Shakespeare: Essays in Cultural Materialism.*

Ed. Jonathan Dollimore and Alan Sinfield. 2nd ed. Manchester: Manchester UP, 1994. 18–47.

Grene, Nicholas. *The Politics of Irish Drama: Plays in Context from Boucicault to Friel.* Cambridge: Cambridge UP, 1999.

Hadfield, Andrew. '"Hitherto she ne're could fancy him": Shakespeare's "British" Plays and the Exclusion of Ireland.' *Shakespeare and Ireland: History, Politics, Culture.* Ed. Mark Thornton Burnett and Ramona Wray. New York: St Martin's, 1997. 47–67.

———. '"The Naked and the Dead": Elizabethan Perceptions of Ireland.' *Travel and Drama in Shakespeare's Time.* Ed. Jean Pierre Maquerlot and Michele Willems. Cambridge: Cambridge UP, 1996. 32–54.

Healy, Thomas. 'Past and Present Shakespeares: Shakespearian Appropriations in Europe.' *Shakespeare and National Culture.* Ed. John J. Joughin. Manchester: Manchester UP, 1997. 206–32.

Heaney, Seamus. 'The Haw Lantern.' *Selected Poems 1966–1987.* New York: The Noonday Press, 1995. 238.

Helgerson, Richard. *Forms of Nationhood: The Elizabethan Writings of England.* Chicago: University of Chicago Press, 1992.

Henchy, Deirdre. 'Dublin in the Age of O'Casey: 1880–1910.' *Essays on Sean O'Casey's Autobiographies.* Ed. Robert G. Lowery. Totowa, NJ: Barnes and Noble, 1981.

Henry V. Dir. Laurence Olivier. Perf. Laurence Olivier, Freda Jackson, and Nicholas Hannon. Paramount, 1944.

Henry V. Dir. Kenneth Branagh. Perf. Kenneth Branagh, Emma Thompson, and Derek Jacobi. Samuel Goldwyn Company, 1989.

Highley, Christopher. 'The Royal Image in Elizabethan Ireland.' *Dissing Elizabeth: Negative Representations of Gloriana.* Ed. Julia M. Walker. Durham, NC: Duke UP, 1998. 60–76.

Hogan, Robert and Richard Burnham. *The Years of O'Casey, 1921–1926: A Documentary History.* Gerrards Cross: Colin Smythe, 1992.

Holland, Jack. *Hope Against History: The Course of Conflict in Northern Ireland.* New York: Henry Holt, 1999.

Holloway, Joseph. *Abbey Theatre: A Selection From His Unpublished Journal, Impressions of a Dublin Playgoer.* Carbondale: Southern Illinois UP, 1967.

Hopkins, Lisa. 'Neighbourhood in *Henry V.' Shakespeare and Ireland: History, Politics, Culture.* Ed. Mark Thornton Burnett and Ramona Wray. New York: St Martin's, 1997. 9–26.

Hunt, Hugh. *The Abbey: Ireland's National Theatre 1904–1979.* New York: Columbia UP, 1979.

Innes, C.L. *Woman and Nation in Irish Literature and Society, 1880–1935.* Athens, GA: University of Georgia Press, 1993.

Joyce, James. *Ulysses: The Corrected Text.* Ed. Hans Walter Gabler with Wolfhard Steppe and Claus Melchior. New York: Vintage, 1986.

Kearney, Colbert. 'Sean O'Casey and the Glamour of Grammar.' *Anglo-Irish and Irish Literature: Aspects of Language and Culture*. Proceedings of the Ninth International Congress of the International Association for the Study of Anglo-Irish Literature Held at Uppsala University, 4–7 August 1986. Vol. 2. Ed. Birgit Bramsback and Martin Croghan. Stockholm: Almqvist and Wiksell International, 1988. 63–76.

Kiberd, Declan. *Inventing Ireland*. Cambridge, MA: Harvard UP, 1995.

Kosok, Heinz. *Sean O'Casey, The Dramatist*. Gerrards Cross: Colin Smythe, 1985.

Krause, David, ed. *The Letters of Sean O'Casey, 1910–41*. New York: Macmillan, 1975.

Krause, David and Robert G. Lowery, eds. *Sean O'Casey: Centenary Essays*. Gerrards Cross: Colin Smythe, 1980.

Lim, Walter S.H. 'Figuring Justice: Imperial Ideology and the Discourse of Colonialism in Book V of *The Faerie Queene* and *A View of the Present State of Ireland*.' *Renaissance and Reformation* 19.1 (1995): 45–70.

Loomba, Ania. *Colonialism/Postcolonialism*. London and New York: Routledge, 1998.

McGrath, F.C. *Brian Friel's (Post)Colonial Drama: Language, Illusion, and Politics*. Syracuse: Syracuse UP, 1999.

Maley, Willy. *Nation, State and Empire in English Renaissance Literature: Shakespeare to Milton*. New York: Palgrave, 2003.

Meissner, Colin. 'Wars Between Worlds: The Irish Language, the English Army, and the Violence of Translation in Brian Friel's *Translations*.' *Colby Quarterly* 28 (1992): 164–74.

Mercier, Vivian. 'English Readers: Three Historical "Moments."' *Irish Writers and Politics*. Ed. Okimufi Komesu and Masaru Sekine. Savage, MD: Barnes and Noble, 1990. 3–35.

Metford, J.C.J., ed. *The Dictionary of Christian Lore and Legend*. London: Thames and Hudson, 1983.

Mikhail, E.H. *The Abbey Theatre: Interviews and Recollections*. Totowa, NJ: Barnes and Noble, 1988.

Moran, Sean Farrell. *Patrick Pearse and the Politics of Redemption: The Mind of the Easter Rising 1916*. Washington, DC: Catholic University of America Press, 1994.

Morash, Christopher. *A History of the Irish Theatre 1601–2000*. Cambridge: Cambridge UP, 2002.

Moryson, Fynes. *An Itinerary*. London, 1617.

Murphy, Andrew. *But the Irish Sea Betwixt Us: Ireland, Colonialism and Renaissance Literature*. Lexington: UP of Kentucky, 1999.

——. 'Shakespeare's Irish History.' *Literature and History* 5 (1996): 38–56.

Murray, Christopher. 'The "Might of Design" in *The Plough and the Stars*.' *Irish Writers and Politics*. Ed. Okifumi Komesu and Masaru Sekine. Savage, MD: Barnes and Noble, 1990. 223–36.

Neill, Michael. 'Broken English and Broken Irish: Nation, Language, and the Optic of Power in Shakespeare's Histories.' *Shakespeare Quarterly* 45.1 (1994): 1–32.

Norden, John. *Speculum Britannia*. London, 1598.

O'Casey, Sean. *Juno and the Paycock. Three Plays*. New York: St Martin's, 1957.

———. *The Plough and the Stars. Three Plays*. New York: St Martin's, 1957.

Parker, Patricia. 'Uncertain unions: Welsh leeks in *Henry V*.' *British Identities and English Renaissance Literature*. Ed. David J. Baker and Willy Maley. Cambridge: Cambridge UP, 2002. 81–100.

Patterson, Annabel. *Reading Holinshed's Chronicles*. Chicago: University of Chicago Press, 1994.

Payne, Robert. *A Brife Description of Ireland*. London: Thomas Dawson, 1590.

Pearse, Padraic. *Collected Works of Padraic Pearse: Political Writings and Speeches*. Dublin and London, 1922.

Porter, Raymond J. 'O'Casey and Pearse.' *Essays on Sean O'Casey's Autobiographies*. Ed. Robert G. Lowery. Totowa, NJ: Barnes and Noble, 1981. 89–102.

Quinn, D.B. *The Elizabethans and the Irish*. Ithaca, NY: Cornell UP, 1966.

Rackin, Phyllis. *Stages of History: Shakespeare's English Chronicles*. Ithaca, NY: Cornell UP, 1990.

Rees, Joan. 'Shakespeare's Welshmen.' *Literature and Nationalism*. Ed. Vincent Newey and Ann Thompson. Liverpool: Liverpool UP, 1991. 22–40.

Rich, Barnabe. *A New Description of Ireland*. London, 1610.

Richtarik, Marilyn J. *Acting Between the Lines: The Field Day Theatre Company and Irish Cultural Politics, 1980–1984*. Washington, DC: Catholic University of America Press, 2001.

Robinson, Lennox. *Ireland's Abbey Theatre: A History 1899–1951*. London: Sidgwick and Jackson, 1951.

Roche, Anthony. 'A Bit Off the Map: Brian Friel's *Translations* and Shakespeare's *Henry IV*.' *Literary Interrelations: Ireland, England and the World--II: Comparison and Impact*. Ed. Wolfgang Zach (intro.) and Heinz Kosok. Tubingen: Narr, 1987. 139–48.

Saccio, Peter. *Shakespeare's English Kings: History, Chronicle, and Drama*. Oxford: Oxford UP, 1977.

Said, Edward. *Culture and Imperialism*. New York: Vintage, 1993.

———. *Orientalism*. New York: Vintage, 1978.

Saxton, Christopher. *Atlas of England and Wales*. London, 1579.

Schrank, Bernice. '"There's Nothin' Derogatory in th' Use o' the Word": A Study in the Use of Language in *The Plough and the Stars*.' *Irish University Review* 15.2 (1985): 169–86.

Shakespeare, William. *The First Part of Henry the Fourth*. 1596. *The Riverside Shakespeare*. Ed. G. Blakemore Evans. Boston: Houghton Mifflin, 1974. 847–81.

———. *The Second Part of Henry the Fourth*. 1598. *The Riverside Shakespeare*. Ed. G. Blakemore Evans. Boston: Houghton Mifflin, 1974. 886–923.

———. *The Life of Henry the Fifth*. 1599. *The Riverside Shakespeare*. Ed. G. Blakemore Evans. Boston: Houghton Mifflin, 1974. 935–71.

———. *The Tragedy of Hamlet, Prince of Denmark*. 1601. *The Riverside Shakespeare*. Ed. G. Blakemore Evans. Boston: Houghton Mifflin, 1974. 1141–86.

———. *The Tragedy of King Richard the Second*. 1596. *The Riverside Shakespeare*. Ed. G. Blakemore Evans. Boston: Houghton Mifflin, 1974. 805–37.

———. *The Tragedy of Othello, the Moor of Venice*. 1604. *The Riverside Shakespeare*. Ed. G. Blakemore Evans. Boston: Houghton Mifflin, 1974. 1203–40.

Shapiro, James. *Shakespeare and the Jews*. New York: Columbia UP, 1996.

Sidney, Sir Philip. *Discourse on Irish Affairs*. London, 1571.

Silverstein, Marc. '"It's Only a Name": Schemes of Identification and the National Community in *Translations*.' *Essays in Theatre* 10 (1992): 133–42.

Spenser, Edmund. *A View of the Present State of Ireland*. 1596. Ed. W.L. Renwick. Oxford: Clarendon, 1970.

Synge, J. M. *The Playboy of the Western World*. *The Playboy of the Western World and Riders to the Sea*. 1907. New York: Dover, 1993. 1–57.

Tatham, John. *The Scotch Figgaries*. In *The Dramatic Works of John Tatham*. New York: Benjamin Bloom, 1967. 115–87.

Tazón-Salces, Juan E. 'Politics, Literature and Colonization: A View of Ireland in the Sixteenth Century.' *Dutch Quarterly Review of Anglo-American Letters* 18.3 (1988): 186–98.

Toynton, Evelyn. 'Themselves.' *The American Scholar* 62 (1993): 283–90.

Travers, Pauric. 'The Priest in Politics: The Case of Conscription.' *Irish Culture and Nationalism, 1750–1950*. Ed. Oliver MacDonagh, W.F. Mandler, and Pauric Travers. New York: St Martin's, 1983. 121–36.

Walker, Julia M., ed. *Dissing Elizabeth: Negative Representations of Gloriana*. Durham, NC and London: Duke UP, 1998.

Yeats, William Butler. *On Baile's Strand*. 1904. *Irish Drama 1900–1980*. Ed. Cóilín D. Owens and Joan N. Radner. Washington, DC: Catholic University of America Press, 1990. 42–65.

Index